KIRK DOUGLAS

KIRK DOUGLAS

A Pyramid Illustrated History of the Movies

by
JOSEPH McBRIDE

General Editor: **TED SENNETT**

PYRAMID
PUBLICATIONS
NEW YORK

To Irene Forrest

KIRK DOUGLAS
A Pyamid Illustrated History of the Movies

A PYRAMID BOOK

Copyright © 1976 by Pyramid Communications, Inc.

Pyramid edition published June 1976

Library of Congress Catalog Card Number: 00-0000

Printed in the United States of America

Pyramid Books are published by Pyramid Publications (Harcourt Brace Jovanovich). Its trademarks, consisting of the word "Pyramid" and the portrayal of a pyramid, are registered in the United States Patent Office.

PYRAMID PUBLICATIONS
(Harcourt Brace Jovanovich)
757 Third Avenue, New York, N.Y. 10017

Layout and Design by ANTHONY BASILE

ACKNOWLEDGMENTS

My editor on this project, Ted Sennett, was a bulwark of strength, and other valuable assistance came from Nancy Belle Fuller, who did a substantial amount of research in the files of the Academy of Motion Picture Arts and Sciences; Patrick McGilligan; Gerald Peary; Karyn Kay; Todd McCarthy; and Paul Lynch. Thanks also to the staff of the Academy library and to Barbara Kaiser and her staff at the State Historical Society of Wisconsin, which houses the extensive and invaluable collection of Kirk Douglas' papers.

Photographs: Jerry Vermilye, the Memory Shop, Cinemabilia, Gene Andrewski

CONTENTS

A figure from a romantic novel at one moment, a Dostoevskian anti-hero the next, Kirk Douglas is a complex, volatile mass of contradictions. His phenomenal energy and intensity is his most readily identifiable characteristic, spilling over from his roles into his professional life off-camera, making him fight as hard as the *Champion* for the films he believes in making. "I've always tried to retain what I call an amateurish feeling about making movies," Douglas said in 1960, during the making of his mammoth $12,000,000 production, *Spartacus*. He had become a producer in the mid-fifties "in self-defense," not content with mere stardom, but wanting to exercise pervasive control over his film vehicles.

More recently, though with less success so far, Douglas has tried his hand at directing, yet it is difficult to escape the conclusion that he has been a true *auteur*, an actor-*auteur*, since he first achieved star status with *Champion* in 1949. Like any other star, he has sometimes been trapped in shoddy vehicles, to keep his name before the public or his finances in shape, but his list of credits contains a relatively high proportion of committed, personally expressive films. "I've always shot my mouth off about story," he remarked once, and an inspection of his personal and corporate papers (preserved in a large

INTRODUCTION: THE FIGHTER

collection he donated to the State Historical Society of Wisconsin) shows that he has always worried over minutiae of characterization at every step of the filmmaking process, from initial broaching of the idea, through script development, during shooting, and into the stages of post-production and marketing.

"I've always insisted on voicing my suggestions with directors," he adds. "The good ones have never objected. I find the secure person will listen to you and be open, but the insecure man is fighting for his own dominance, and he's afraid that accepting another person's point of view will weaken him." It takes a strong director to face up to a feisty actor like Kirk Douglas, but he has always sought out strong collaborators, even when, as in the case of *Spartacus*, one tough director (Anthony Mann) has wound up being replaced by another (Stanley Kubrick), while Douglas has remained in charge.

"With some stars this would be a detriment," Kubrick said at the time, "but in the case of Kirk, who has great taste and intelligence and integrity, he makes an ideal producer."

The maverick quality in Douglas' career is something which was ingrained in him from early youth.

As Vincent Van Gogh in LUST FOR LIFE (1956)

His life as the son of impoverished, illiterate Russian-Jewish immigrant parents has seemed like a Horatio Alger story, "so corny," he has said on many occasions, "as to be unbelievable." Yet the life vein running through virtually all of his films is a spirited, anguished critique of the American success ethic. The fighter in *Champion* (the prototypical Douglas role), the heartless reporter in *Ace in the Hole*, the violent cop in *Detective Story*, the megalomaniacal film producer in *The Bad and the Beautiful*, his tormented Van Gogh in *Lust for Life*, the conscience-stricken military officer in *Paths of Glory*, the savagely idealistic liberated slave in *Spartacus*—all of these highlights in Douglas' career have the common characteristic of fusing animal vitality, clawing-to-the-top fierceness, with a deep-seated, often guilty awareness of the cost of worldly success.

Elia Kazan, who directed Douglas in the confused yet powerful adaptation of *The Arrangement*, remarked that Douglas is "a very hardworking, intellectual guy who is not happy about his own career." It is this ambivalence, this paradoxical sense of failure in the midst of glorious achievement, that gives Douglas' career its peculiar vitality and power.

Douglas is a charming, urbane, kind, warm man; yet he has also been regarded by many in Hollywood and elsewhere as an SOB ("I've never won any popularity contests," he admits), ruthlessly pursuing his own vision at the expense of others' feelings. What he wrote of Kubrick in a 1957 letter could also be applied, to some degree, to himself: "He is a very talented fellow, but needs a lot of help, much more help than he cares to admit." The obvious contradictions in his personality are what make him respected, if not always loved, in an industry which too often breeds a sheeplike docility in even its most successful inhabitants. A pensive man despite his hyperactivity, a well-read man, a political liberal, and an old-fashioned believer in American ideals without subscribing to naive idealism or jingoism, Douglas has always tried, within the limits of commercialism, to work on films which engage both his mind and heart. He states his attitude toward power in terms many of his characters could endorse: "I think half of the success in life comes from first finding out what you really want to do, and then going ahead and doing it."

To some segments of the filmgoing public, Douglas is synonomous with the jut-jawed, strident-voiced, tirelessly pugnacious characters he usually plays on screen (his gentler characters, such as the English professor in *A Letter to Three Wives* or the alienated cowboy in *Lonely Are the Brave*, are somehow seen

As Jack Andrus in TWO WEEKS IN ANOTHER TOWN (1962)

as less typical), and the *Harvard Lampoon*, an undergraduate humor magazine known for its sophomoric irreverence, voted him its worst actor award three years in a row during the 1950s, finally retiring it as the "Kirk Douglas Award."

More intellectual critics have frequently shared this opinion—Manny Farber, while writing for *The Nation* in the early fifties, used to give out a facetious "Oscar" award which he dubbed "The Emanuel," describing it as a "celluloid statue of Kirk Douglas, ranting"—and perhaps it is Douglas' very intensity, his lack of "cool," that has encouraged a derisive response from his detractors. "I don't *try* to be intimidating," he insisted a few years ago. "In fact, I know that if I express an opinion vehemently, the person who is listening loses track of whether I'm right or wrong. My *presentation* loses the argument. I've been guilty of that often. But the problem is, I'm never content to be just an actor. I want a chance to express my opinions."

Douglas always cares, on screen and off, and he always throws everything into his material, even if it is beneath his best instincts. No one has ever accused him of walking through a part, unlike, say, Robert Mitchum, who has made a career of being blasé and ironic toward his vehicles, turning himself into a cult figure while accumulating a generally inferior list of credits.

An early biographical article described the typical Douglas character as that of "the neurotic heavy, the man with a baleful obsession—essentially weak or unsavory but with such understandable motivation as to evoke a degree of sympathy." The latter quality is clearly attributable to Douglas' intelligence; he is never a stupid or unfeeling heavy. Even in commercial tripe like *Once Is Not Enough*, the 1975 adaptation of Jacqueline Susann's novel, Douglas maintains a measure of integrity and dignity by investing his character with an awareness of his own culpability and degeneration. Both as an actor and as a producer-director, he has always searched for stories which allow him to express a believable ambivalence.

It is interesting to compare memos Douglas wrote to directors planning what eventually became two of his best films, Billy Wilder's *Ace in the Hole* and Stanley Kubrick's *Paths of Glory*. Of the reporter in Wilder's film, undoubtedly the heaviest heavy he has ever played, Douglas told Wilder, "He must have an interest in some character other than himself. . . . I feel that all the characters in the newspaper office must really enjoy this guy Chuck, and appreciate his ability." Conversely, while playing a relatively sympathetic role in

As Frank in THE BROTHERHOOD (1969)

Paths of Glory, Douglas was afraid of making him "too sanctimonious and a sort of Prince Valiant type. He lacks an ironic humor that must be injected into his character, and there is constantly that pitfall of a guy who is much too noble." Few stars are so articulate, or so concerned with bringing out the gray areas in their characterizations.

His initial attempts at directing, *Scalawag* (1973) and *Posse* (1975), were both commercially unsuccessful (though *Posse* received some excellent reviews), and lately Douglas has been turning his sights more to television acting and producing. He said once that he was preparing himself for the day when his star would begin to fade, the day when he would continue to exert his force as a filmmaker by moving behind the camera. Though, in his sixtieth year, he is in remarkable physical shape, still as ruggedly powerful-looking as ever (perhaps even more interesting as an actor with the addition of more lines and maturity), he is, however, once again at a turning point in his life. But Douglas has always thrived on crisis, and it's hard to conceive of him ever giving up.

"All my life," he once said, "the thing that's turned out best for me is the thing that someone has been saying 'Don't do.'" If he had listened to his agents, he wouldn't have done *Champion*, but would have continued his gradual, carefully planned climb towards stardom in a lavish MGM production, *The Great Sinner*, with Gregory Peck and Ava Gardner. Instead, he turned down the part, doing *Champion* for a modest $15,000 and a gambler's share of the profits, because the film "just had a kind of smell to it." Of course, he was right, as he has been while taking many other seemingly dubious steps in his career. While making *Spartacus*, probably the most artistically satisfying of all his own productions, he noted that the film was considered "sheer madness" by most people in Hollywood. After it was finished, he commented with satisfaction, "*Spartacus* has a lot of the elements of *Champion*."

"Full of *chutzpah* and class," as Stanley Kramer once said, Douglas will never let go of an idea, even a wrong one, and it is that fierce dedication that makes a study of his career decisions so rewarding. For an actor to achieve such a measure of control over his career is a rarity in Hollywood, and Douglas has reason to look back over his career with as much pride as discontent. It is the mark of an intelligent man, after all, never to be fully satisfied, and Douglas is, as Elia Kazan testifies, "the most intelligent actor I've ever worked with."

Kirk Douglas' climb to success as a man and an actor illuminates many aspects of his films. His parents came to the United States in 1910, by steerage, to escape the cycle of poverty and persecution and realize their dream of the New World. "You see," Douglas said years later in a homecoming speech, "every success, success of any kind, stems from a dream." Yet there was also frustration at the end of the rainbow—Douglas' father was never able to achieve a satisfactory career and finally left the family, letting his wife raise their son and six daughters.

Douglas was born Issur Danielovitch on December 9, 1916, in Amsterdam, New York, a small industrial town in the Mohawk Valley known for its carpet and rug industry. At the time his parents immigrated, more than 100,000 Jews were leaving Russia for the U.S. each year, many, including Douglas' father Herschel, to avoid military conscription. The roots of his social convictions are clearly here. In 1905, the New York *Evening Post* commented, "Russia, while denying her Jewish subjects all civil rights, does not object to sending them to Manchuria to stop Japanese bullets. For the Jew, however, even military glory is denied, as he is not permitted to rise in the ranks. It is not strange, therefore, that the war does not arouse any

WHY HE FIGHTS

sentiments of patriotism and that he should instead think it a particularly auspicious time to seek the land of freedom."

Herschel Danielovitch has been described by his son as "a personable and physically powerful man but totally unskilled and confused in his efforts to make a living." Working as a peddler with a horse cart, and sometimes collecting junk, Herschel didn't make enough money to feed the family properly, and Douglas went to work at an early age, selling soda pop and candy to the men in the mills. Before becoming a professional actor, he eventually held more than forty menial jobs, and today it is little wonder that he is unable to be complacent about money and success.

"There's a tendency to romanticize these things," he has remarked of that struggling period. "I'm against a boy having to work his way through school the way I did. It's a waste of precious time for him to be working part-time as a waiter or a gardener. All his time should be spent working on his studies and on sports, and some real fun and relaxation. I find my own sons much more informed than I was at their age, much more aware of life. It took me years to concentrate on being a human being."

His mother Bryna, after whom he later named his production company, was perhaps the dominant influence in his life, instilling him with the importance of achieving an education and fighting for independence both spiritually and financially: "My mother once told me she literally expected to find gold bricks in the streets of America. These were the kinds of myths that they grew up on, but later she said she'd found something more valuable—the idea of a country where her son was able to work his way through college, get a degree, and pursue the work he'd selected to do." Bryna also had "very strong anti-Russian feelings," and made her son promise not to go to Russia until after she died.

Douglas fondly remembers a telephone conversation he had with Bryna not long after he came to Hollywood. "Ma," he said, "I just signed a million-dollar contract." She replied, "That's nice, but you know, I saw you in that last picture. You looked very *thin*."

His father was less encouraging, more reticent, perhaps less eager to pass on his own frustrated hopes to the son. After Douglas did *Champion*, and returned to Amsterdam feeling triumphant, he asked his father, "Did you see the picture?" Herschel (by then Harry) shrugged, "Yeah, yeah." Douglas prodded,

With his school team, top row, second from the left

As a young actor

"Did you like the picture?," and his father just said, "*Yeah*, yeah." Douglas recalls sadly, "All I wanted him to say was, 'Boy, you're terrific.'" His second wife, Anne, in a 1962 *Saturday Evening Post* profile of her husband, wrote that part of what motivates him is "a monstrous effort to prove himself and gain recognition in the eyes of his father. The old man is dead now—he died in 1954—but the pattern was set early, and not even four years of psychoanalysis could alter the drives that began as a desire to prove himself." These feelings later found vivid expression in Douglas' relationship with Richard Boone in *The Arrangement*, frantically seeking love from his dying, irascible father.

It was his English teacher at Wilbur Lynch High School, Louise Livingston, who first encouraged Douglas to follow an acting career, and also brought out his feelings for literature, continuing Bryna's work in encouraging him to go to college. One special eye-opener was a field trip on which the teacher took Douglas and other students to see Katharine Cornell on stage in *The Barretts of Wimpole Street*, and he nurtured his dramatic talents by appearing in school plays and oratorical contests. After going to Hollywood, Douglas kept up a correspondence with Livingston, and at one point, when she experienced financial hardship, he bought a short

story from her, ostensibly as a film project.

Douglas' sisters stayed home and supported the family so that he could go to college at St. Lawrence University in Canton, New York. "Many times I felt a little guilty about this," he has admitted, and Anne Douglas feels her husband has always "needed to get away from female domination." Certainly women have influenced Douglas' character at many crucial stages of his life.

He arrived at college, colorfully enough, on the back of a fertilizer truck, smelling strong, with $163 in his pocket, and convinced the dean to give him a loan and a job as a janitor. Douglas, who wrestled on the college team, also did some wrestling in a carnival. "I guess I really learned to act in the wrestling ring," he told John L. Scott of the Los Angeles *Times* in a 1948 interview. "I was the hero of the act. The villain, wearing a black hood, would stalk around the ring hurling challenges at the audience. I would pretend to be a spectator, then start arguing with the bruiser and finally crawl into the ring, strip down to my wrestling costume, and throw him. The crowds thought it was strictly legitimate." The experience later came in handy as background for *Champion*, but he avoided telling his family about the job, afraid it would upset them.

In 1939, Douglas went to Green-

An early portrait

wich Village and entered the American Academy of Dramatic Arts. In college, as he recalled in a 1966 *Redbook* interview, he had wanted to be a poet. "I used to wear my shirt open down the front and write a lot of poetry. And it was a shocking day when I suddenly realized that all the poetry I ever wrote was rather mediocre. And if there's anything that I hate, it's mediocrity. So that ended the career of a mediocre poet."

Among his few social acquaintances at the Academy (where he was remembered as "a quiet, friendly boy who worked very hard") were Betty Perske, later to be known as Lauren Bacall, and the aristocratic, Bermuda-born Diana Dill, whom he married in 1943. "I used to follow Diana around just to hear her talk," he recalls. He picked the name Douglas because of Douglas Fairbanks, and Kirk because it seemed "snazzy."

Summer stock jobs eventually led to a break on Broadway, when producer Guthrie McClintic cast him as a singing telegram boy in *Spring Again*, a 1941 production which starred Grace George and C. Aubrey Smith. His second Broadway role, in Katharine Cornell's *Three Sisters*, was equally inauspicious—he played an off-stage echo. His line was "Yo-ho."

The war interrupted his career, and he enlisted in the Navy after being turned down in his request to be an Air Corps pilot. It was his characteristic ability to see things three-dimensionally which made him fail the test; he was told, "You evaluate too carefully, you weigh all the pros and cons. We need instantaneous decisions."

Wounded in the South Pacific, Douglas was given a medical discharge in 1944 and returned to New York, where he replaced Richard Widmark in the juvenile lead of *Kiss and Tell*, which led to jobs in radio and two unsuccessful plays, *Trio* and *Alice in Arms*. He was called "tolerably good" in the latter, but Howard Barnes of the New York *Herald Tribune* wrote of his next role, the Unknown Soldier in *The Wind Is Ninety*, that while the part was "impossible," "Douglas plays it with a jaunty grace that endows it with dignity and feeling."

Bacall recommended Douglas to Hal B. Wallis, the Hollywood producer, who offered him a screen test. Still bent on a stage career, he refused, but reconsidered when *The Wind Is Ninety* closed, and was cast by Wallis in a 1946 film, *The Strange Love of Martha Ivers*. One more stage role that year, in *Woman Bites Dog*, was his last contact with the theater until 1951, when he played *Detective Story* in Phoenix to prepare for the film role. By then, he had made it in Hollywood.

In his film roles before *Champion*, Douglas became typed as a neurotic weakling, because of his debut in *The Strange Love of Martha Ivers*, which, he observed in a 1950 interview, "almost killed me off professionally . . . when my name was brought up for stronger roles, producers would say no." The weakling image was, of course, diametrically opposite to the one he would later develop, and after *Champion*, he began such an aggressive pursuit of tough-guy roles that his publicists warned him against playing a Nazi in the early fifties, for fear it might alienate the public just when he was becoming a major star.

Martha Ivers had him playing the cowardly son of a working-class opportunist. Douglas marries the corrupt Barbara Stanwyck, and through her connection is appointed district attorney, only to find himself mired in deeper corruption. It was a lurid film, though meticulously directed by Lewis Milestone, who had made *All Quiet on the Western Front*, and critics praised Douglas for making the weakling sympathetic. "I thought it was a wonderful role and I played it very well," Douglas told *Films and Filming* in 1972. "Now if I play a weak character, I try to see where he's strong, and if I play a strong character, I try to see where he's weak. But the public types you,

MAKING·IT

nevertheless—they say, *that's* the way you are."

Douglas was pleased to be directed by Milestone, but he recalls that he "didn't know enough to be awed." He learned a valuable lesson from the veteran director while doing a test scene for the part. Seeing that Douglas was nervous, Milestone said, "Well, Kirk, let's just run through it again, and the extra run-through will relax you and then we'll shoot it." They did it again, and Milestone asked, "Are you ready now?" Douglas said he was, and the director replied, "Well, go home. I've already shot it." From that, the actor learned the importance of relaxing in front of the camera, not feeling intimidated by it, and not being self-conscious. "What Milestone did for me," Douglas recalls, "was the most marvelous thing for somebody just starting out in movies—the lesson being to forget that the camera is there."

Martha Ivers, which was called *Love Lies Bleeding* before it went into production, is a prime example of the misogynistic trend of American films just after the second World War, when movies entered what historians now call the *"film noir"* period—black, bleak, pessimistic films full of neurosis, social disintegration, and senseless

THE STRANGE LOVE OF MARTHA IVERS (1946).
With Barbara Stanwyck

THE STRANGE LOVE OF MARTHA IVERS (1946).
With Barbara Stanwyck

violence. It was a curious contrast, in a way, to the generally upbeat mood of the country following the war, with the economy still riding the crest of war production and patriotism in triumphant ascendancy. But under the surface, tensions were boiling up, veterans were having trouble readjusting and finding jobs (as *The Best Years of Our Lives* so memorably conveyed that year), and marriages were straining under the pressure of delayed reunions. The year 1946 was, until 1974, the biggest boom year for movie attendance in the history of the American film industry, and Douglas benefited from both the new resurgence in filmmaking and the darkened postwar mood that would eventually enable him to express many of the anxieties befalling the country.

His second film, *Out of the Past* (1947), is considered a classic *film noir* by historians today, and director Jacques Tourneur has acquired a higher reputation, in retrospect, than he had at the time. Andrew Sarris, in *The American Cinema*, praises Tourneur's direction of *Out of the Past* for its "civilized treatment of an annihilating melodrama." The source for the film was a Geoffrey Homes novel, *Build My Gallows High*, and Douglas was cast as a high-powered gangster, ruthless and amoral.

One reviewer caught something Douglas had brought to the role which few, if any, other actors would have contributed. Douglas "obviously did not come up from the ranks of ordinary mobsters," the reviewer noted. "A man of considerable charm and refinement, he is a little difficult to suspect of nefarious activities, but that only makes his involvement in them more intriguing."

Douglas was not the lead — that part went to Robert Mitchum, excellent as a compromised former private dick frustrated by Douglas in his attempt to go straight—but the role helped show he could do more than just play the craven weakling. Today, the film retains its fascination because of Tourneur's typically well-designed atmospheric shooting, his careful accumulation of mood details, and the stylish playing of the principals, including Jane Greer as one of the classic villainesses of *film noir*.

A more obviously ambitious project, RKO's adaptation of Eugene O'Neill's tragedy *Mourning Becomes Electra* (1947), was, all things considered, a disappointment for Douglas, and his acting in a minor role, as he later wrote in a letter, "did nothing to alleviate" the film's failure. The film ran three hours in its original release (later cut) and was directed, adapted, and produced by Dudley Nichols, one of Hollywood's finest screenwriters, perhaps best known for his adaptation of *The Informer* and for

OUT OF THE PAST (1947). With Robert Mitchum

other work with John Ford.

In O'Neill's drama, modeled on the Greek tragedy, *Electra*, Rosalind Russell had the central role of Lavinia Mannon, the passionately obsessed daughter of a high-bred New England family (circa 1865). Douglas played a young army officer in love with her—another rather spineless part, but as the New York *Daily News* observed, "The smiling, open face of Kirk Douglas as Lavinia's fiancé is an effective contrast to the dark complexities of the other characters, until he, too, is altered by the tragedies."

The film failed dismally at the box office, even though critics generally praised the full-blown performances of the cast, which also included Michael Redgrave, Raymond Massey, Katina Paxinou, and Leo Genn, fine company indeed for young Douglas so early in his film career. What usually happens when "prestige" stage vehicles are translated to film occurred with this one—the public went to sleep. And the viciousness of the characters didn't help; with some irony in its lack of historical perspective, *Liberty* magazine pointed out, "Not even Lillian Hellman ever thought up a family as unpleasant as the Mannons."

Hal Wallis then put Douglas into another of his productions in 1947, a deservedly little-remembered gangster movie called *I Walk*

MOURNING BECOMES ELECTRA (1947). With Rosalind Russell and Michael Redgrave

MOURNING BECOMES ELECTRA (1947). With Rosalind Russell

I WALK ALONE (1947). With Burt Lancaster

Alone. It was the second picture in what was then a five-film deal between Douglas and Wallis, but Douglas understandably got out of his contract after this turkey, in which he was paired for the first time with Burt Lancaster.

They played a pair of old rum-running buddies reunited after Lancaster returns from a long prison stretch to find Douglas, whose rap he had to take; Douglas is now running a fancy night club with Lizabeth Scott as vocalist. Predictably, Scott changes her affections and helps Lancaster get rid of Douglas. *The Hollywood Reporter* felt that Douglas "dominates every scene by the sheer force of his underplaying"—a talent not much noted in later stages of his career, but evident enough when seen in conjunction with the teeth-baring flamboyance of Lancaster. Both men were reported to be dissatisfied with Wallis and the project, trying to make script changes and unhappy with their pay, and a Hollywood columnist referred to Douglas and Lancaster as "the terrible twins."

Douglas next played an ambiguous but far from heelish role in *The Walls of Jericho* (1948), an early 1900s soap opera which cast him as a small-town newspaper publisher embroiled in a rivalry with pure-hearted lawyer Cornel Wilde. Some of Douglas' interest in political themes came out in muted form here, and it's revealing that twenty-seven years later, under his own direction in *Posse*, he also played a political opportunist (a sheriff) who similarly inflames puritan morality for the sake of his own rising career. But Douglas doesn't remember *The Walls of Jericho* with any fondness; in 1960, when asked to list his favorite and least favorite films, he said he was proudest of *Lust for Life*, *Paths of Glory*, *The Bad and the Beautiful*, and *Cham-*

pion, and least fond of *Mourning Becomes Electra*, *The Walls of Jericho*, *My Dear Secretary*, *Along the Great Divide*, and *The Big Trees*.

He noted wryly that it was the "curse of television" that kept bringing these duds back to haunt him, something which had never occurred to actors making routine bread-and-butter vehicles in the forties. What, at the time, might have seemed an acceptable stepping-stone to a better part looms in retrospect as a shameful blot on a career. It's important to see these middling films as part of an overall career pattern, realizing that no

THE WALLS OF JERICHO (1948). With Linda Darnell

actor is fully in command of his roles at any stage of his career, even though Douglas and others have tried to achieve such control.

In *My Dear Secretary* (1948), Douglas tried to broaden his range by doing his first film comedy, playing an eccentric *bon vivant* novelist who finally settles down with Laraine Day, only to be up-staged when she becomes a more successful writer. In an interview many years later in the Los Angeles *Times*, Douglas succinctly analyzed the film's failure: "I tried to play Cary Grant but wasn't Grant."

As if by some malevolent fate warning him not to overstep his bounds as an actor, when Douglas tried another romantic comedy, *For Love or Money*, in 1963, Bosley Crowther scolded in *The New York Times*: "Kirk Douglas might do better sticking to Westerns and rallying Roman slaves than to try to bull his way through the fragile crockery of Cary Grant's type of comedy." Douglas has never found the proper vehicle for the charming, debonair side of his personality, which he has had to be content with expressing in the more benign moments of his dramatic roles.

One of the screen's masters of civilized, sophisticated comedy is

MY DEAR SECRETARY (1948). With Laraine Day

A LETTER TO THREE WIVES (1948). With Linda Darnell and Thelma Ritter

Joseph L. Mankiewicz, whose flair for barbed, sparkling repartee has brightened such films as *All About Eve*, *The Barefoot Contessa*, and *The Honey Pot*, as well as his sixth film, one of his best, *A Letter to Three Wives* (1948). Douglas was cast, against his emerging tough-guy image, as a serious, idealistic English teacher uncomfortably married to Ann Sothern, who drives him up the wall with her writing of radio soap operas. It was a sympathetic role, light-years more sophisticated than the not totally dissimilar character he had played in *My Dear Secretary*, and it gave him the chance to vent some personal feelings about the plight of underpaid teachers in the United States. Later, while discussing the film before a group of teachers, Douglas became so upset about the problem that he started haranguing them, as if *they* were the enemy. He joked about the experience, but it was typical of his penchant for expressing his private feelings in public at the drop of a hat.

The film also had much to say about American marital mores, for

A LETTER TO THREE WIVES (1948). With Jeanne Crain and Ann Sothern

Mankiewicz examined with great wit and incisiveness the social fabric of the town in which Douglas and Sothern live, commenting on each of the title's three women by showing how their aspirations conflicted with those of their husbands. For Jeanne Crain and Jeffrey Lynn, the problem was depicted through the wife's insecurity and possessiveness, and for Linda Darnell and Paul Douglas, the wife's desire for material comforts emphasized the superficiality of her marriage to a wealthy businessman.

Time especially liked the section with Kirk Douglas and Sothern, saying the scenes had "a strong satiric bite . . . a more realistic standard." Douglas must have been particularly pleased with the *Variety* review, for it gave him points for believable human comedy touches in the midst of an essentially sober portrayal. *The Hollywood Reporter* gave the film a rave, saying that Mankiewicz' "lines are razor-sharp; the situations incisive; and the touches show a sense of human foibles with which the spectator can only too readily identify himself."

CHAMPION (1949).
As Midge Kelly

Champion in 1949 brought Douglas his first Academy Award nomination—he was nominated again for *The Bad and the Beautiful* and *Lust for Life*—and paid off the gamble he had taken in turning down the $50,000 offer from MGM to play in *The Great Sinner*. Producer Stanley Kramer, then in the process of establishing himself as a Hollywood "whiz kid" before going on to a career as the foremost exponent of message movies, was among the most successful independent producers in the late forties and early fifties, following his *Champion* success with such offbeat films as *Home of the Brave*, *The Men*, *Death of a Salesman*, and *High Noon*. But when *Champion* was made, he, like Douglas, was pushing hard for a name and for the respect of Hollywood.

The production cost of *Champion* was a modest $589,801, made possible by careful pre-planning and rehearsal. Director Mark Robson, who had started in the Val Lewton B-picture unit at RKO, was skilled at cutting corners, and he utilized all of his Lewton training to the fullest advantage in Douglas' first screen breakthrough, the tale of a ruthlessly ambitious prizefighter, adapted by Carl Foreman from a Ring Lardner short story. If some of its elements seem overly clichéd today—as do, indeed, certain aspects of the more sophisticated *Body and Soul*, made in

1947—it is because these films, and *The Set-Up* (another 1949 boxing picture, directed by Robert Wise, also a Lewton alumnus), set a mold which many films have since followed.

"Kirk Douglas, who has been edging himself rapidly up the stellar ladder, completes the climb with his performance of the *Champion*," *The Hollywood Reporter* proclaimed, and other reviewers were equally ecstatic. The Los Angeles *Times* said Douglas was "grinning, cocky, and quite irresistible"; *Look* called his performance "rousing" and said he "becomes an important screen star overnight"; and *Variety* said his "grim and deadly [portrayal] and the manner in which he handles himself in the ring gives evidence of a thorough prepping job, for the fights are frighteningly realistic."

Though he had wrestled in college, Douglas had never boxed before doing *Champion*, and he said he had "three left hands" then, but trained intensively for weeks until he became, in his own modest description, "a passable fighter."

He later applied the same careful research to other roles, studying aerial gymnastics for *The Story of Three Loves*, juggling for *The Juggler*, police work for *Detective Story*, and newspaper reporting for *Ace in the Hole*. In his 1957 *Saturday Evening Post* two-part autobiographical series ("as told to"

CHAMPION (1949). With Arthur Kennedy and Paul Stewart

Pete Martin), Douglas commented:

"It could be that my willingness to work long and hard to master a new skill is just another manifestation of my hamminess—a desire to create a sensation with an unexpected accomplishment; then throw it away by saying, 'It's really nothing.' But I honestly don't think that's it. It's not so much exhibitionism on my part as a need to believe in those games of 'let's pretend.' If I believe in them hard enough, moviegoers may believe in them too."

Douglas' belief in "childlike" behavior as an actor resulted in one of the most memorable scenes in *Champion*. At the end, just before he dies, his character goes berserk in the locker room and smashes his hand into a metal locker door, holds the hand up incredulously for his manager to inspect, and then dies. Playing the scene, Douglas recalled something his son Joel had done when he cut his finger as a baby, holding it out and saying, "Daddy, Daddy." So in the locker room, when his hand is smashed, Douglas looks at his manager, Paul Stewart, and says, "Tommy, Tommy." It was a devastatingly powerful emotional moment, because, as Douglas observed, "in any real emotion you revert to a childlike quality."

The character of the boxer Midge Kelly—seen developing in flashback from the ring in which he is at the most triumphant moment of his career—enabled Douglas to analyze the self-destructive, guiltily voracious qualities he would later find in so many of his screen characters. Midge not only risks his life by fighting mob domination (a staple in fight stories), he callously discards his first manager on the way to the top, cuckolds his second manager, and, in the *pièce de résistance* of brutalism, slugs his crippled brother (Arthur Kennedy) when the hitherto adoring fellow dares to criticize his new mode of conduct.

Most reviewers and fans were so enraptured by Douglas' animal vitality in the role that they overlooked the nuances of characterization he and Robson added to make the fighter's villainy credible. Perhaps the most interesting critique of the film, in *The New Yorker*, spotlighted this side of the film, though it did so to compare it unfavorably with the Lardner story:

"Lardner told the story of . . . a heel who was no good from the day he first drew breath. Now, in a movie adaptation of the story, Midge is revealed to be a victim of circumstance. He is a heel, all right, but he gives indications every now and then of having a finer side—a side that the buffetings of poverty have compelled him to suppress.

"He doesn't knock his mother out, as he did when he was Lardner's boy; instead, he contributes to her welfare. And far from belting his crippled brother as a kind of going-away present when leaving home, he looks after the boy and doesn't let him have it until goaded unmercifully. I think *Champion* would have been a better picture all around if the producers had stuck to the letter of the original and not tried to find justification for a monstrous human being, but these may be merely the strictures of a Lardner purist."

Actually, Lardner purists notwithstanding, it is hard not to wonder what would have happened had Douglas played the character as a total monster. He would have blown himself off the screen—and probably would have made the character a caricature of villainy, rather than a human being with tragic flaws. Here, as so often, Douglas can be seen shading the gray areas with careful strokes, even in the midst of the most headspinning, gut-crunching action.

Midge Kelly also gave Douglas an opportunity for his first full-scale masochistic characterization. Like Marlon Brando, he seems to relish getting beaten up and humiliated on screen in exaggeratedly brutal ways, perhaps as an antidote to the character's overreach-

CHAMPION (1949). With Paul Stewart

Kirk Douglas at home

On the set of THE BIG TREES (1952) with sons Michael and Joel

ing ambition—the more he reaches, the worse he must be chastened.

When Douglas emerged a star from the film, Hollywood observers were quick to find parallels between Midge and Douglas' own battling personality, often caustically, as Hollywood is wont to do. The powerful columnist Hedda Hopper said to him, "You know, Kirk Douglas, you've changed. This *Champion* has really gone to your head, you know. You're such an SOB now."

Douglas retorted with glee, "You're mistaken. I was an SOB *before Champion*, but you never noticed it."

His marriage to Diana broke up that year (the couple had two children, Michael, now an actor and producer, born in 1944, and Joel, born in 1947), but Douglas insisted it wasn't a result of his new prominence, only the inevitable outcome of pressures that had been building up for some time. His second wife, Anne, feels the fact that both Kirk and Diana were actors caused an unhealthy rivalry between them. She adds, "I believe one of the reasons Kirk married me was that I was not an actress and had no desire whatever to be one."

In his *Post* autobiography, Douglas reflected somberly on stardom and its responsibilities, contending, "I think I'm still the way I was before *Champion*. I didn't kowtow to producers then; I'm not noted for it now. Even when I was a bum, standing in line on the Bowery to buy a cheap Salvation Army meal, I didn't buddy up to people I thought were jerks, no matter how much good they could do me. This is not always the accepted way to get ahead. Too often in the entertainment field, the idea persists that you can ignore influential creeps only after you become successful."

But in an interview five years later, he mused, "Very often the tragedy of success is that it's the fulfillment of a dream, and in the fulfillment of a dream you lose the dream."

When *Champion* had a sneak preview, Douglas was surprised to find people rushing at him, demanding autographs as he left the theater. "I remember being a little bit sad and thinking to myself, 'Gee, I'm a star.'"

After *Champion*, Douglas experienced the heady, potentially destructive situation of being a suddenly hot "property." It's said that success in Hollywood comes at the moment when people you have been trying to reach on the telephone now start calling you—and that, in essence, was Douglas' situation. Everyone wanted him, and he had to sift the offers, take and reject advice on business matters, and still, as he always had done, keep his own counsel about what direction to follow.

His agent at the time was the late Charles K. Feldman, a tough, flamboyant Hollywood character who later became a successful producer. Douglas signed with Feldman's Famous Artists Corporation in 1946, staying with Feldman until 1958, when he became disgruntled and went to MCA and Lew Wasserman (now board chairman of MCA, which has expanded into a conglomerate controlling, among other interests, Universal Pictures). He later switched to the William Morris Agency, which represents him today.

At the time he left Famous Artists, Douglas wrote Feldman, "Maybe I am a difficult client, and it is possible, as some people seem to think, that I am too demanding." His letters during the period 1949-1958 included frequent gripes against his agents (who included

THE FRUSTRATIONS OF STARDOM

Ray Stark, now a producer) for not working hard enough to secure unusual roles for him. This is a common complaint of actors, even in the case of stars, and despite Douglas' dissatisfaction, his files are also filled with lengthy and regular letters from Stark outlining possible projects and evaluating many of the interesting scripts going around town.

Feldman persuaded Douglas to sign a long-term contract with Warner Brothers after *Champion*, guaranteeing him $900,000 for nine films in seven years. Douglas later called it a "very bad piece of advice," and he managed to break the contract in 1952, after three films, by offering to do *The Big Trees* for nothing ("it was a terrible film," he remarks). The other films Douglas did for Warners were *Young Man With a Horn* and *The Glass Menagerie* in 1950, and *Along the Great Divide* in 1951, none of which he considered satisfying. Interspersed with them were two considerably more interesting films for Paramount in 1951, Billy Wilder's *Ace in the Hole* and William Wyler's *Detective Story*. Douglas was particularly incensed when Warners tried to prevent him from being in *Detective Story*, a role he coveted.

In 1950, Douglas was nominated

YOUNG MAN WITH A HORN (1950).
As Rick Martin

as best actor for his performance in *Champion* but he lost to Broderick Crawford in *All the King's Men*. In a letter dated March 30, 1950, a week after the Oscar ceremony, Douglas wrote, "I was not in the least low about the Academy Awards. Although I was happy that there might be a slight chance of my getting it, when the whole thing was over, I had nothing but a wonderful feeling of relief."

Young Man With a Horn, Douglas' first film after *Champion*, didn't hurt his career; in fact, it was a solid, serious role, that of a jazz trumpeter (modeled on Bix Beiderbecke), sliding into alcoholism after marriage to a confused, rich woman, Lauren Bacall. The story had some resemblances to *Champion*, though Douglas was a much more sympathetic character; it was told in flashback, as fellow musician Hoagy Carmichael reminisces about Douglas' climb to the top from an impoverished beginning. *The Hollywood Reporter* said Douglas ''gives a performance approximating in dramatic intensity his tour de force in *Champion*. A bit zealous at times but, in this particular role, it is all to the good.''

Michael Curtiz, who directed *Casablanca* and scores of other popular cynical-romantic melodramas, did his customary slick and expert job of direction. Doris Day was also in the film, singing a few memorable numbers including "With A Song In My Heart," and Harry James did Douglas' trumpet work while the actor mimed his routines. Douglas practiced for three months on the trumpet to prepare for the part, and *Variety* praised him for "clever fingering and lip technique."

The screenplay, by *Champion* scenarist Carl Foreman with Edmund H. North, from a novel by Dorothy Baker, reprised some elements from the earlier film which had already been done with greater force, and in that respect, the film seems both derivative and less exciting. For instance, Douglas

YOUNG MAN WITH A HORN (1950). With Doris Day

YOUNG MAN WITH A HORN (1950). With Lauren Bacall

THE GLASS MENAGERIE (1950). With Jane Wyman

smashes his trumpet at a low point in his career (after he has failed in his persistent attempt to hit an elusive high note), an action similar to his self-destructive fist-smashing scene in *Champion.* Douglas later drew a connection between the two scenes, observing in an interview that to a fighter, his fist is his "instrument." Warner Brothers had been sitting on the novel for five years, and it was only Douglas' sudden prominence that prompted producer Jerry Wald to activate the project.

After the film was finished, Douglas wrote in a letter that it was "a source of great frustration that this picture did not turn out to be

the movie it could have been." But the feeling of the role lingered with him; when composer Johnny Green sent a condolence wire to "my favorite trumpet player in Hollywood" after Douglas lost the *Champion* Oscar, the actor replied, "I haven't been working in several months now, and since pictures have been so hard to get, I have been working on my trumpet."

Douglas said that most of the scripts he was reading then were "crap." Within a year, he was even more frustrated. When Stanley Kramer offered him a role in *The Four Poster,* Douglas replied, "My first reaction is that I wouldn't be suitable for the part, but, after months of reading scripts, I'm beginning to think that I'd be the last to know what part I am suited for."

The Glass Menagerie seemed like a promising film, and Douglas had the secondary but piquant role of the "Gentleman Caller" who brings a few moments of gentle romance into the blighted life of the crippled Laura, played by Jane Wyman. Playwright Tennessee Williams—who based the work on his sister's experiences, and put himself into the play as her brother Tom (played in the film by Arthur Kennedy)—also worked on the film script, but somehow the genteel, reverent approach of director Irving Rapper didn't make the play come alive as a first-rate film. Maybe such "prestige" enterprises are doomed to failure, as was *Mourning Becomes Electra*, for a play is conceived as a confined vehicle with horizons limited by the proscenium arch, and it is only the rare good play, or the mediocre one, which can be transformed into effective filmmaking.

The reviews at the time were quite good, though, and Gertrude Lawrence won some kudos for her work as the addled mother, Amanda Wingfield. (*The New York Times* dissented, however, calling her performance "the fatal weakness of the film.") *Newsweek* commented that Douglas, "the friend wise enough to know a

ACE IN THE HOLE (1951). With Bob Arthur

crippled leg doesn't have to mean a crippled life, guides (Wyman) out of her morass of insecurity with just the right amount of shyness and inarticulate conviction."

Those qualities were decidedly absent from Douglas' next role in the vitriolic *Ace in the Hole*, Billy Wilder's attack on mob psychology and the heartless desire of newspapermen to get a story, even at the expense of human lives. It is still one of the blackest, most uncompromising films to come out of Hollywood, and director Samuel Fuller, himself a former newspaperman, has called Douglas' role "the best portrayal of an SOB reporter ever put on screen."

Loosely based on the Floyd Collins cave-in incident of the twenties, which created a flurry of national publicity, *Ace in the Hole* is about a down-and-out reporter, Chuck Tatum, who winds up on a small paper in Albuquerque, New Mexico, after being fired from a string of Eastern papers for insubordination, hell-raising, and a score of other offenses against propriety. Seething with bitterness, and grasping at any straw which

ACE IN THE HOLE (1951). With Jan Sterling

will take him back to the top of his profession, Tatum comes across a man trapped in an underground cave and ruthlessly keeps the man imprisoned while pretending to mastermind the rescue operation. After a week, the man dies, and Douglas has his scoop, but he pays for it with his life when the dead man's sluttish wife, played with icy callousness by Jan Sterling, shoots him. Douglas staggers back into the newspaper office and falls at the feet of editor Porter Hall, saying, "How would you like to make yourself a thousand dollars a day, Mr. Boot? I'm a thousand-dollar-a-day newspaperman. You can have me for nothing."

Years later, Douglas said that the screenplay—by Wilder with Lesser Samuels and Walter Newman—was the best he had ever had in his career: "Aside from making a suggestion or two which (Wilder) could either accept or reject, it was completely out of my hands. I think that's a wonderful luxury. But generally speaking, you don't get it very often, because you don't get such a script."

In his memo to Wilder, dated June 19, 1950, Douglas thought the script could be improved by injecting a bit of human fellow-feeling into Tatum's relationship with his colleagues on the newspaper, and specifically objected to the tenor of a particularly vicious scene in which Tatum gives a long monologue con-trasting the sophistication of New York with the deadness of Albuquerque. The suggestions were not taken by Wilder, but it is intriguing to see what bothered Douglas about this "conceited monologue with macabre overtones":

"It is too early in the story for the audience to have a resentment toward Chuck Tatum which they very easily could have. The guy's been given a job there even if he doesn't like it. He's been working with these people for a year, and all he does, in a very superior way, is knock everything about their place. To the copy boy he says, 'When the history of this sun-baked Siberia is written, these shameful words will live in infamy: No pastrami! No garlic pickles! No Lindy's! No Madison Square Garden! No Yogi Berra!'

"I honestly feel, Billy, that there should be some amusing way for his expressing his need for pastrami and garlic pickles which represent his home that could be done in a way which would show a kind of relationship between them. . . .

"Next, what the hell is Yogi Berra? I asked several people who don't know, and now I must admit that my secretary, who is taking this down, is amused that I don't know. She says that he's a catcher. I may be in a very small minority as far as Yogi is concerned, but my point still is, Billy, that he mustn't take out on these people his restless

51

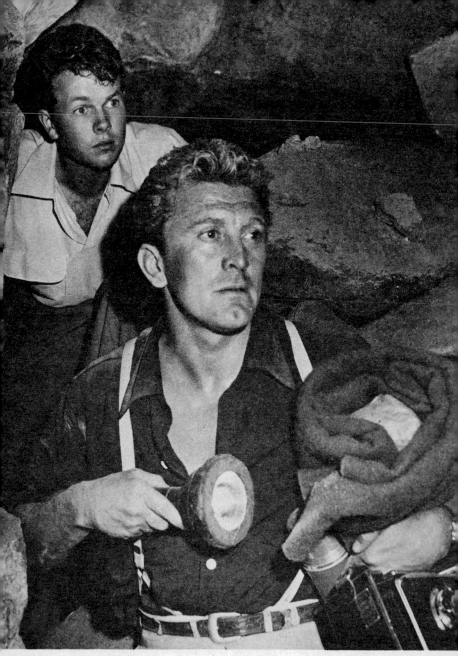

ACE IN THE HOLE (1951). With Bob Arthur

desire to get back .... Because to me, this scene is the springboard of the story, and if the audience buys Chuck Tatum in this scene, they'll buy him in anything else that he does later on, no matter how dastardly."

The generally appalled reaction to the film proved Douglas right in a box-office sense, for audiences found it hard to identify with the character of Tatum. The film was a failure, and was finally retitled *The Big Carnival* by Paramount in a desperate attempt to make it sound like "fun." Douglas' commercial instincts, stemming from his professional concern with communicating his inner feelings to an audience, in this case were stronger than Wilder's, but the film is so powerful that in the final analysis Wilder may have been right in trying to make a statement with absolutely no concessions to popular taste.

What made the film especially unpalatable to the public, no doubt, was Wilder's contemptuous depiction of the crowds who flock to the cave-in sight and turn it into a carnival, complete with merry-go-round, refreshment stands, and a country singer warbling a song called "We're Coming, Leo." The public correctly perceived that they were the true heavies in the story, and a further problem hampering the film's reception was the outraged response of many newspaper critics who objected to the Tatum character.

Bosley Crowther in *The New York Times*, while calling the film "one of the truly challenging pictures of the year ... so forceful in its own brash, intense, insulting way," also said that Wilder's attitude toward journalism was "cynical and misleading." *The Hollywood Reporter* called the film "a brazen, uncalled-for slap in the face of two respected and frequently effective American institutions, democratic government and the free press ... Kirk Douglas' conception of a reporter is overbearingly arrogant and made more ludicrous by the hammy histrionics."

Chagrined by the general response to the film, Wilder (who now calls it, with affection, "the runt in my litter") was beginning to wonder if the film wasn't unfair to the press until he left his office the day the reviews appeared and witnessed an auto accident. As he went to help the injured person lying in the gutter, a newspaper photographer came up and took a picture. Wilder asked him to help, but the photographer said, "Sorry, buddy, I've got a deadline," and ran off. After that, Wilder knew his film was telling the truth.

"When in doubt, make a Western," John Ford once remarked, and Douglas took that advice by following *Ace in the Hole* with his first cowboy picture, *Along the*

Around 1951

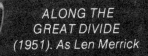
ALONG THE
GREAT DIVIDE
(1951). As Len Merrick

DETECTIVE STORY (1951). With Luis Van Rooten and William Bendix

Great Divide, a minor but not uninteresting film directed by veteran Raoul Walsh, one of Hollywood's foremost action directors. Douglas played a U.S. marshal who saves Walter Brennan (excellent, as usual) from a lynching and eventually exonerates the old man after a long, eventful trek into town. It was a routine story, but Walsh brought some of his typical blustery charm to it, and the film had a convincingly rugged atmosphere.

Before doing *Ace in the Hole*, Douglas had put in a stint as a reporter on the Los Angeles *Herald and Express*, finally getting a byline on a story about a child who had accidentally swallowed poison, and

in preparing the film adaptation of Sidney Kingsley's play *Detective Story*, he hung around New York's 16th precinct police station, soaking up atmospheric details of the cop's life. He was so taken with the experience that he asked director William Wyler to let him change the squad's number in the film from 21 to 16.

The role was another in Douglas' gallery of obsessive, near-psychopathic characters, this time in the person of Detective James McLeod, described by Manny Farber as "a one-man army against crime . . . an authoritarian sadist." McLeod is prone to using his fists on crooks, and he has a particularly

DETECTIVE STORY (1951). With Horace MacMahon and Eleanor Parker

vehement hatred for abortionists, typified in the film by George Macready, but because of censorship, the role was changed somewhat mysteriously into that of a man who runs a home for unwed mothers and then disposes of the infants. When McLeod finds that his wife (Eleanor Parker) once had dealings with Macready, he suicidally allows himself to be shot, in an ending somewhat similar to that of *Ace in the Hole*.

Certainly, it was all highly melodramatic, but Wyler's highly polished direction and the sophisticated camerawork of Lee Garmes, coupled with the acting of a fine cast, aided greatly in making it a first-rate piece of hokum, far above the run of the usual cops-and-robbers movie. Since the play deals with one "typical" day in the life of the precinct police, Wyler decided to confine it as much as possible to a single set, without much "opening up," and the decision heightens the claustrophobic tension which finally leads Douglas to explode.

As a further means of getting into the mood for the role, Douglas arranged for a stage production of the play in Phoenix, Arizona, away from the prying eyes of Hollywood, but, as he recalls, "Suddenly, the thought of going on stage again frightened me. I hadn't worked in front of a live audience in a few years, and I started to get tense . . . . I lost my voice." He was replaced by another actor, and, as if by magic, his voice "started to come back. On opening night the people in the back row heard me loud and clear." Wyler watched his performances and took notes which later helped him direct Douglas in the film.

As he had done with Wilder, Douglas wrote a memo to Wyler commenting on the script (this was before doing the play). In the memo he said that his main criticism of the play was the same as that expressed by critic Ward Morehouse, who wrote, "*Detective Story* is probably more convincing in its fascinating and photographic detail than it is in its main story line."

Douglas told Wyler, "I, too, am excited at the theme of a man who is right to a fault, of a man who prejudges others and destroys himself. Because of too many stories, the relationship between McLeod and his wife seems a little weak. Mr. Kingsley misses the opportunity of showing more of the softer and more human side of McLeod's nature in contrast to the hard, intense fanatic he is at his work. We could give McLeod more humor which would add variety to the characterization and point up more sharply his inner conflict. The lightness in a more developed relationship would also relieve what would otherwise seem an overly grim and sordid story."

DETECTIVE STORY (1951). With Eleanor Parker

Some of this came across in the film, and as *Variety* noted, Douglas brought "a spark of compassion" to the character which made the finale closer to tragedy than to melodrama. But Crowther, like some other reviewers, found the film "more skillful than profound . . . just a melodramatic tour de force."

Working with Wyler, one of Hollywood's most prestigious and also most authoritarian directors, caused Douglas some initial problems. As he wrote in a letter to Wyler after the filming, "For the first few days, you had me completely baffled. You seemed to be wrapped in an impenetrable shell, and I'm a guy who needs a very personal contact. But once, when you didn't know it, you had your guard down, and I saw under it a very warm, human person with the sense

DETECTIVE STORY (1951). The climax: Kirk Douglas confronts Joseph Wiseman.

of humor of a kid who likes to throw bags of water from a second story window on the unsuspecting pedestrians below. This won me over completely, and for this I forgive all the whiplashes across the back that you gave me during the course of the picture." Douglas signed the letter "your devoted slave," and though the experience of working with Wyler was never repeated (Douglas turned down a secondary role in *Ben-Hur*), it was a valuable one in his development.

Douglas next turned his attention to trying to purchase film rights for Clifford Odets' play *The Country Girl*, the story of an alcoholic actor and his wife, eventually played by Bing Crosby and Grace Kelly when Paramount made the film in 1954 (Kelly winning an Oscar). Douglas' idea, outlined in a letter to Ray Stark on January 30, 1951, was to buy the play in conjunction with Odets and two other top stars on a cooperative basis, do it as a play first as he had done with *Detective Story*, and then do it as a movie "for a fantastically low sum and on a quick shooting schedule." It never panned out, and when Crosby played the role, the character was changed to a singer. Interestingly, Douglas, who has described himself as a "frustrated bathroom

THE BIG TREES (1952). With Edgar Buchanan (on ground)

THE BIG TREES (1952). With Patrice Wymore

baritone," often sought singing roles in later years until he finally did a musical version of *Dr. Jekyll and Mr. Hyde* on television in 1973.

Ever persistent, he managed to have songs inserted into several of his films—but failed to land the lead in *Pal Joey*, losing it to Frank Sinatra. Also, because of schedule conflicts, he was unable to accept producer Harold Prince's offer in 1965 of playing Tevye on stage in *Fiddler on the Roof.* Prince had written him, "Word reaches me that you sing fine . . . I think you would be marvelous," and Douglas replied, "I'm glad word of my vocal powers has finally reached the East Coast. I could never understand why Lerner and Loewe chose Rex Harrison instead of me" (for the Henry Higgins role in *My Fair Lady*).

The Big Trees, ending Douglas' period of servitude at Warner Bros. and marking the last time he would ever subject himself to a studio contract, was a feeble story about a 1900 con-man who tries to make a fortune from exploiting California redwood trees, but eventually has a change of heart inspired by his contact with the religious sect which owns the land.

It was a fittingly lackluster end to his period as a company man, before the drive toward independence which would eventually lead, in 1955, to his forming of Bryna Productions. In an unpublished 1960 interview, Douglas looked back on some of his unpleasant experiences as a star, venting the frustrations which still go along with success:

"It's lonely being an actor. Goddam lonely. Being an actor in the sense of being a so-called star, to arrive somewhere and it's a goddamned sharp pinnacle . . . All your life you've been dreaming of wanting to act, to portray roles. Then what happens is that if you're successful at it, you become big business. A myriad of things that you never bargained for come into play. All of a sudden you are buffeted from every side and you're fortunate if you're a guy who has the right advice. Look at the disastrous experiences *I've* had with bad business management advice, bad lawyers who put me into all kinds of ridiculous situations for their own personal gain and to my detriment. I think it is just that we are so damned under the influence of people who have our ear."

When Howard Hawks made *Red River*, with John Wayne, he had an idea for a scene in which Wayne's finger would get mangled between a rope and a saddle horn. The cowboys would get Wayne drunk, amputate the finger, and then he would scramble around looking for it so he could "go to heaven whole." Wayne was aghast, asking Hawks, "What kind of scene is that?" Hawks replied, "It's supposed to be funny." When Wayne insisted it wasn't funny, Hawks said, "All right, I'll do it with somebody who's a better actor."

In 1952, when he made *The Big Sky* with Douglas, Hawks found the actor who could do the scene. And a memorable scene it was, too, with Douglas' drunken giddiness changing abruptly to childlike anguish as he frantically crawls through the dust, whimpering, "Where's my finger? I gotta find my finger." Hawks' eccentric sense of humor, coupled with Douglas' offbeat approach to character, had made the bizarre scene work. Wayne saw the film and told Hawks, "If you say a funeral is funny, I'll do a funeral."

The Big Sky is a very uneven film, rambling and spacious, a talltale adventure recalling the Western stories of Mark Twain at its best moments and, in weaker spots, marred by obvious studio settings and long stretches of adoles-

CONSOLIDATING A CAREER

cent fistfights and corny theatrics. But there is some genuine grandeur in the film's awestruck gazing at the beauties of the Grand Teton National Park, and in the majestic course of a keelboat up the river, conveyed with Hawks' typical close attention to the details of how things are done and how men make their living. Douglas played a bumptious, boisterous frontiersman named Jim Deakins in this adaptation (by Dudley Nichols) of a novel by A. B. Guthrie, Jr., and though Hawks never had the skills in handling large-scale outdoor action that John Ford had, the director managed to invest the story with plenty of colorful character detail and feeling for picaresque group activity.

Douglas accepted the part after securing Hawks' agreement that the scenes between his character and that of his companion, Boone (played by Dewey Martin), would be rewritten to beef up Deakins' part. Like many other Hawks films, the story is basically a "love story between men," with a woman (an Indian played in mysteriously beautiful fashion by Elizabeth Threatt) coming between them and causing a painful rupture in their relationship. The film ends almost

THE BIG SKY (1952). With Dewey Martin

tragically, as the men are separated when Threatt chooses Martin over Douglas, and Douglas returns to his wandering life on the river. By the end, both men seem to have grown up, having come to a mature understanding of their need for women's companionship.

Because it was based on a relatively prestigious novel, *The Big Sky* was accorded unusually favorable reviews for a Western. *The Saturday Review*, for example, noted rather snobbishly that the film "represents a step forward for Hollywood . . . though replete with Indians, buffalo, and Western scenery [it] is more than a Western. It explores a real tradition, and becomes almost the first true Hollywood attempt to equate, with some honesty, the events with the

THE BIG SKY (1952). With Arthur Hunnicutt (left)

geography." Douglas also had fine notices, *Variety* calling his performance "one of his best . . . a sincere characterization, equally impressing whether the scene is drama, comedy or action."

One of the highlights of the film was an early scene in a tavern in which Douglas, slightly drunk, sings "Whisky Leave Me Alone" in stylish hipster fashion to Boone and an obliging barmaid, then gets embroiled in a fight which is unexpectedly, and hilariously, terminated when he is knocked cold with a metal bar tray. It's a raucous, jaunty performance, even if Douglas' constant ear-splitting smile, baring a wider expanse of teeth than Burt Lancaster could ever manage, occasionally makes the spectator wonder how he avoided giving his mouth muscles a Charley horse.

After six years in Hollywood, Douglas had accumulated an intensive first-hand knowledge of the ruthless, hard-boiled business dealings which go on behind the scenes, and his performance as producer Jonathan Shields ("I'm gonna ram the name of Shields down their throats") in *The Bad and the Beautiful* (1952) was, as *Newsweek* observed, "close to perfection in a part calculated to make almost any Hollywood actor wince while he works."

Originally called *Tribute to a Bad Man*, and intended for Clark Gable, who turned it down, the John Houseman production was one of the best of all Hollywood-on-Hollywood exposés. It showed how Douglas, in a pattern becoming familiar to his films, rose to fame and riches while destroying the lives of several people who were closest to him personally and professionally. In this case, the victims were memorably played, under Vincente Minnelli's deft direction, by Lana Turner (as an actress modeled on Diana Barrymore), Walter Pidgeon (an unflappably genteel producer), Barry Sullivan (an unfairly treated director), Dick Powell (a writer who, in the best tradition of Hollywood myth, sells his soul for money), and Gloria Grahame (winning an Oscar for her comic playing of Powell's neglected wife, a Southern belle with calculatedly "cutesy-poo" mannerisms).

The Shields character was partially taken from aspects of the careers of David O. Selznick (for the megalomaniacal traits) and Val Lewton (for the imaginative corner-cutting techniques in low-budget filmmaking), but Douglas imbued it with his by now characteristic blend of *chutzpah* and wracking self-disgust. He has the magnetism and charisma in the role which makes it entirely plausible for Turner and the others to follow him down the road to destruction, while still being fully aware of his utter

THE BAD AND THE BEAUTIFUL (1952). As Jonathan Shields

selfishness. Bosley Crowther, who had high praise for the verisimilitude of the film's details, commented in *The New York Times*, "Kirk Douglas is best as the producer—a glib, restless, unrelenting gent whose energies and resources are matched only by his perfidy and gall ... Granted that the producer is an extreme and eccentric type, he is nonetheless realistic and reflective of many legends of 'genius.' "

What the film may have lacked in depth it certainly compensated for in sheer entertainment value, and Minnelli managed to draw from Turner a performance that few then thought her capable of giving. In her scenes with Douglas—which gave Douglas the chance to rant his head off while still remaining in the bounds of believable characterization—Turner projected a world-weary sophistication, bred of alcoholism, too many career-building degradations, and an obsessive devotion to the memory of her late actor-father. Douglas cruelly smashes up her shrine-like mementoes of her father, then takes her in one of the classic love-combined-with-loathing romantic clinches. The film ends with Douglas, off-screen, once again wheedling Pidgeon, Turner, and Powell into yet another business deal; it's a cleverly executed ending to a film which is sure enough of itself to inject a constant strain of ironic humor, never taking itself too seriously.

"*The Bad and the Beautiful* was a wonderful job on Minnelli's part," Douglas commented to a *Films and Filming* interviewer in 1972, "because it's very difficult to make a film about filmmaking. Somehow you'd think it would be easy for filmmakers to do that, but most of the attempts seem false, and I thought *The Bad and the Beautiful* was an exception: a pretty honest movie."

Houseman was dismayed when MGM imposed the title of *The Bad and the Beautiful* on the film—since Turner received top billing, it could hardly be called *Tribute to a Bad Man*, the rationale went—but after the film became a popular success and won five Academy Awards, he began to think it wasn't such a bad title after all. Douglas was nominated for best actor, but lost again, this time to Gary Cooper in *High Noon*, which also took the best picture award.

His next film, also for MGM, was one episode, called *Equilibrium*, in a three-part film, *The Story of Three Loves* (1953), which was titled *Three Love Stories* before going into production. Douglas was teamed with Pier Angeli as a trapeze artist and a girl who becomes his partner in the act after he saves her from committing suicide. Yet again, the stories were introduced via flashback, with all of

THE BAD AND THE BEAUTIFUL (1952). With Lana Turner

the principals first seen on a liner. Douglas brought conviction and some degree of depth to his role, a typically determined character whose ambition turns to self-loathing after he causes the death of an earlier aerial partner.

Stanley Kramer reteamed with Douglas for a low-budget 1953 film, *The Juggler*, shot on location in Israel, which received critical praise but didn't make much impact at the box office. Douglas was a former juggler, a German Jew, who journeys to Israel after becoming mentally unbalanced by seeing his wife and two children killed in a Nazi concentration camp. After almost killing an Israeli policeman, whom he thinks is a Nazi storm trooper, Douglas becomes a fugitive again. He is finally saved from destruction by the love of a young Israeli widow, Milly Vitale, who helps him recover his juggling skills and start to recover his sanity. It was a film for which both Douglas and Kramer had high hopes—Kramer originally intended to direct, then wanted Fred Zinnemann, finally settling on the mediocre Edward Dmytryk—and Douglas, playing a Jew on screen for the first time, clearly took a

THE BAD AND THE BEAUTIFUL (1952). With Lana Turner

THE STORY OF THREE LOVES (1953). With Pier Angeli

deep personal interest in the project.

Location work was arduous, and as a *Variety* writer reported, "Kirk Douglas has been working as hard as any actor I have ever seen. Be it running up alleys that start at about 70 degrees, 20 and 30 takes, and climbing Israeli mountains, making personal appearances where 5-6,000 people almost tear his clothes off, he manages to keep a cheery and excited attitude towards his work and his people."

Like other Hollywood stars at the time, Douglas was concerned about the large bite of his income taken by taxes, and around this period in the early fifties he and others spent much of their time making films in Europe, to take advantage of tax deductions then allowed for prolonged absence from the United States. Another of these was *Act of Love*, a less-than-successful 1953 film, made in France, which is important to Douglas now mostly because he met his current wife while making it.

Anne Buydens, born in Belgium, was hired by producer-director Anatole Litvak to do publicity on the film. As she recalls, "When I

THE JUGGLER (1953). With Oscar Karlweis and Milly Vitale

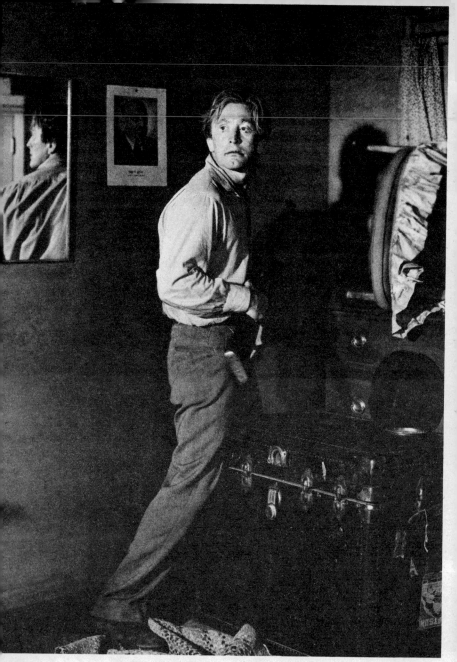

THE JUGGLER (1953). As Hans Muller

With his second wife Anne, arriving in Paris

ACT OF LOVE (1953). With Dany Robin

heard that the star was Kirk Douglas, I wondered if something had happened to Litvak's good taste. While crossing the Atlantic on a boat, I had seen Kirk in a picture called *The Big Trees*. It was so terrible everybody was laughing. But Litvak was an old friend, and I decided to take the job." Her first impression of Douglas was of "the most forceful, energetic and demanding man I ever had met," and the romance began after the filming had gone on for a while, with Douglas typically taking charge of events in a brash, peremptory fashion that she even-

tually found enchanting, after she "began to see this overpowering man in an altogether different way."

They weren't married until sixteen months later, on May 29, 1954, after she had done publicity work on Douglas' next film, *Ulysses*, and he had begun work in Hollywood on a Disney film, *20,000 Leagues Under the Sea*. Today Anne Douglas is a prominent Beverly Hills socialite, spending much of her time on such activities as charity fund-raising and art collecting (as well as taking a venture into producing with *Scala-*

wag, her husband's 1973 directing debut). She and Douglas have two sons, Peter, born in 1955, and Eric, born in 1958.

In *Act of Love*, written by Irwin Shaw from a novel by Alfred Hayes, Douglas is an ex-GI who revisits the French Riviera and, in flashback, remembers his ill-starred romance with a French refugee girl, Dany Robin, during the war. His memories are painful, and as *The Hollywood Reporter* put it, "the performances are constantly moving, Douglas punching over his role with a fierce intensity skillfully softened by tenderness." But today it seems an overwrought tale, full of heavy emphasis, turgid in too many spots.

Ulysses (1954), an adaptation of Homer's *Odyssey* done in the florid toga-and-tunic style of Italian melodrama, was a major disappointment for Douglas, and the troubles began with the script, credited to a slew of writers including Ben Hecht and Irwin Shaw. The muddle that emerged, thanks to the machinations of producers Dino De Laurentiis and Carlo Ponti, bore little resemblance to Homer's classic; remove Homer's name, and the Paramount release could be any other fair-to-middling pseudo-epic made haphazardly in the fifties. Douglas wears a look of palpable upset, almost embarrassment at times, as he grimaces through the unfortunate film, which was directed by Mario Camerini.

In a memo to De Laurentiis, written in France on April 3, 1953, Douglas expressed dismay over two scripts he had been submitted for *Ulysses*, which he said was "a picture that in all honesty I was quite frightened about in the beginning." He told the producer that the scripts were "completely disjointed and completely lacking to my mind in a proper character development on the part of Ulysses and Penelope" (played by De Laurentiis' wife, Silvana Mangano). And Douglas added:

"To me, if you forgive my saying so, both of these scripts had many of the elements of pretentious Hollywood movie-making which does not interest me. To me a story line must be very simple, and when you are dealing with a classic by all means one must avoid the danger of becoming pompous and symbolic to the extent of becoming completely obscure . . . I often thought there was too much dialogue when the action should be told only in pantomime. They explained to me that the entire script is purposely overwritten in many ways to allow the cutting as the story line was sharpened up."

Douglas was also "very shocked" at what he considered the careless shunting-aside of the work done by Hecht. "Frankly," he wrote, "I was delighted when I discovered that you had employed Ben Hecht, and I

ULYSSES (1954). With Silvana Mangano

still cannot understand how after employing a man who not only has written some of the greatest movie scripts but occupies a very high place in American literature, that time was not taken to fully discuss the script ... of course I will be very anxious to read anything your writers are preparing, but who are these geniuses that we must wait for what they have written while we set aside what Ben Hecht has written?"

The Disney film which followed, *20,000 Leagues Under the Sea*

ULYSSES (1954). With Silvana Mangano

20,000 LEAGUES UNDER THE SEA (1954). Ned Land battles the giant squid.

(1954), was of a much higher caliber in all departments, a movie for kids which adults could also enjoy, with a fine, spirited performance by Douglas as harpoonist Ned Land in Jules Verne's tale of Captain Nemo (James Mason, brilliant in his oddly attractive evil) and his 19th-century submarine. Peter Lorre and Paul Lukas also added to the atmosphere of colorful playing and professional craftsmanship, with Richard Fleischer directing Disney's first live-action feature on a $5,000,000 budget. The publicized highlight was the submarine's battle with a giant squid.

Douglas was happy to be back in America for the Disney film, telling Hedda Hopper, "You're looking at a reformed gypsy. I'm footsore from being footloose. I'm tired and happy to be home." From those remarks it sounded like he had engaged in his customary practice, commented on by Anne Douglas, of letting each part "take possession of him." Now he was back from his wandering, like Ulysses, but he disliked having to shave off his beard for *20,000 Leagues*, pointing out, "A beard is great, because it gives a man a hiding place."

After all that, it galled him to have to make his next film, *The Racers* (1955), in Europe. It was a glossy, superficial story about Grand Prix auto racers, routinely directed by Henry Hathaway, a sort of *Champion* or *The Bad and the Beautiful* on wheels, with Douglas playing an ambitious Italian driver hungry for victory at any cost. The film had an international cast and a cacophony of accents; among the principals were Bella Darvi, Katy Jurado, Gilbert Roland, Cesar Romero, Lee J. Cobb, and Agnes Laury. One of the more sympathetic reviewers, Philip Scheuer on the Los Angeles *Times*, felt that Douglas had once again created a lifelike heel: "It is his achievement that though the taut wires that bind him to us snap one by one, one or two are still holding fast at the finish and we are able to rejoice in the discovery that he retains some decent instincts."

Douglas had been trying for several years to get his independent company off the ground, and he finally succeeded in 1955 with *The Indian Fighter*. But before that, he made another Western, *Man Without a Star*, an amiable film directed by King Vidor. Its familiar plot contained some elements common to *The Big Sky* (Douglas and boyish William Campbell as rowdy buddies on the trail), and some which looked forward to an important Douglas film of the sixties, *Lonely Are the Brave*, which also expressed regret and bitterness over the narrowing of the Western frontier. Here, with a script by Borden Chase and D.D. Beauchamp, Douglas played a peripatetic cow-

THE RACERS (1955). As Gino

MAN WITHOUT A STAR (1955). With Jeanne Crain

boy roaming around as the land becomes progressively more civilized, and finally settling on a ranch run by Jeanne Crain, where conflicts ensue with the villainous Richard Boone.

The film was generally well received, with *The Hollywood Reporter* calling it "a personal tour de force of lusty outdoor comedy."

During the making of *Spartacus* in 1960, Douglas told an interviewer, "I think it's a fallacious theory that to do fine things and be a fine actor, you can't make money." That pragmatic sense, coupled with his increasing desire for relative autonomy as an actor-filmmaker, was what led to his activation of Bryna Productions in 1955. "I chose to give it my mother's name," he said, "not just from sentiment but because she was the one who instilled in me this business of gambling on yourself. I once had to tell her, while I was at St: Lawrence, that I had lost some of my hard-earned savings in a card game. She said, 'You're a fool. Why bet money on cards? What do they know about you? What do they care? If you want to bet, bet on yourself.' I found the perfect place to take her advice was in making films."

The monolithic Hollywood studio system began cracking up in the early fifties, largely as a result of the so-called "consent decree" whereby the Supreme Court ruled that studios could not also exhibit their own pictures. (The major studios at the time of the decree also controlled theater chains, and consequently a regular outlet for their films.) It was a spur for independent filmmakers, and there was a dramatic upsurge of production activity by stars in 1955, most-

THE HYPHENATE

ly through deals with United Artists, which had been formed in 1919 by D. W. Griffith, Charles Chaplin, Mary Pickford, and Douglas Fairbanks to distribute their films and those of other actors and directors.

In a March 16, 1955 *Variety* articled entitled "Look, Ma, I'm a Corporation," Douglas was prominently featured among a group of budding actor-producers which also included Frank Sinatra, Cornel Wilde, Robert Mitchum, Joan Crawford, Henry Fonda, and Rita Hayworth with Dick Haymes. All had set up private production companies with deals to produce films released and partially financed by UA. "We're doing it to make money," Douglas told *Variety*, but he added, "In a film, you feel your contribution is less (that that of the director and writer); you want to do more, such as in finding properties and developing them creatively. A lot of us are going to die for one reason or another. I hope it isn't going to be me."

As it turned out, Douglas has been one of the most consistently active actor-producers in Hollywood since 1955 (assisted by Edward Lewis from 1957 through the mid-sixties), while many of the other stars have failed at the so-

MAN WITHOUT A STAR (1955). As Dempsey Rae

THE INDIAN FIGHTER (1955). With Harry Landers and Eduard Franz

called "hyphenate" activity. One major exception during the fifties was Burt Lancaster, a partner in Hecht-Hill-Lancaster, a prominent company which eventually teamed with Douglas to make *The Devil's Disciple* for UA in 1959.

Under tax rules at that time, an actor could save considerable amounts of money by having his company "hire" him at a minimal salary for a film—thus avoiding heavy income taxes—and instead pay his tax at the lower corporate income rate. On gains in company stock, the tax was less than half of the corporate income rate, which was already about half of the individual income tax rate.

Despite the rosy appearance of the tax arrangement, however, producing wasn't always lucrative for Douglas, as he complained in a letter dated June 20, 1960, to Arthur Krim, board chairman of UA. Douglas made four films for UA in the fifties—*The Indian Fighter, Paths of Glory, The Vikings,* and *The Devil's Disciple*—before switching his affiliation to Columbia with *Strangers When We Meet* in 1960, and then to Universal International with *Spartacus* the same year, after the project had been turned down by UA.

Douglas contended he had made "nothing" from UA and had put out considerable amounts of his own money as overhead on the various projects. "I've made many mistakes,'' he wrote Krim. "Sometimes on certain matters advice has been offered to me that I should have accepted . . . I had a terrible deal on (*The Vikings*). I don't blame you. I pay people to advise me, but, in retrospect, I know that my deal was unbelievably bad in comparison to other peoples'. Had *The Vikings* been a bust I would have been in a helluva spot.'' After noting that his advisors told him to reject a UA deal which would have given him a $1,200,000 share of the profits from *The Vikings*—a deal still in negotiation at that time—Douglas concluded, "I just hope you don't all become fat, successful and reactionary. Love, from a lean, unsuccessful liberal.''

Despite his financial problems in the early years of Bryna, Douglas has reason to be proud of most of his work as a producer. Some of his films have been failures both ar-

THE INDIAN FIGHTER (1955). With Elsa Martinelli

tistically and commercially, but others have been substantial successes, and he has been responsible for some unusual, serious work, most notably *Paths of Glory*, *Spartacus*, *Lonely Are the Brave*, and *Seven Days in May*.

The Indian Fighter, directed by Andre De Toth and starring Douglas as a lusty frontier scout and Elsa Martinelli as his Indian lover, was released late in 1955. It was basically a formula picture, with a few unusual slants, on the old theme of war between whites and Indians after unscrupulous traders inflame the Indians with whisky. It was profitable, and established Douglas as a reliable and commercially oriented producer, which is basically what he intended it to do.

The film benefited greatly from its strong production values, which included CinemaScope and color photography of spectacular Oregon locations, and from the practiced, polished scriptwriting of Ben Hecht, who collaborated with Frank Davis. Martinelli, whom Douglas discovered as a fashion model in Italy and put under personal contract, was introduced to the screen in a sexy role.

Douglas' next film, *Lust for Life* (1956), was much more ambitious, befitting another old Hollywood adage, "Take chances only with other people's money." This film biography of Van Gogh, based on Irving Stone's book, was a project Douglas actually had hoped to make for Bryna, but MGM controlled the rights, so he went with them, "rather than buck a company like Metro," as he told *Variety*. Douglas had wanted Jean Negulesco to direct for Bryna, with Norman Corwin writing the screenplay, but as things turned out, Douglas was fortunate to have Vincente Minnelli directing Corwin's screenplay and John Houseman producing. Great care was taken on the production, which was filmed in Belgium, Holland, and France during the summer of 1955, with Freddie Young and Russell Harlan photographing many scenes in a manner approximating Van Gogh's paintings, often on the actual locations which inspired the painter. Though the conception perhaps smacked a bit of middle-brow notions of culture (why should a movie imitate a painting, even if a painter is the subject?), the craftsmanship involved was undeniably first-rate, and the film was widely praised for its color. Unfortunately, the Metrocolor process has proven unstable, and deteriorates badly over the years, so that the prints now available of the film are far below the quality of its original release.

Douglas' close resemblance to Van Gogh was marveled over by most reviewers, and indeed he has said that he first had the idea to do

LUST FOR LIFE (1956). As Vincent Van Gogh

LUST FOR LIFE (1956). With Pamela Brown

LUST FOR LIFE (1956).
As Vincent Van Gogh

the film when he saw a Van Gogh self-portrait and noticed the similarities. Houseman told the Los Angeles *Times* that Douglas regarded the film as "part of his life ... he lives the thing; has read the man's letters, steeped himself in the man."

The violence in this characterization, one of Douglas' finest achievements as an actor, was directed largely inward, rather than against other people, as in the rest of his major performances. Van Gogh's descent from idealistic beginnings into self-destructive madness was powerfully conveyed by Douglas, who plays the role with a sense of lonely, passionate devotion to his craft, capturing the almost evangelical insistence the painter had on communicating through his brush.

The Saturday Review, in a highly favorable review of the film, said it had "a curious, exciting sense of self-revelation as the artist probes the depths of his soul with an ever greater frenzy ... Kirk Douglas' physical resemblance to Van Gogh is extraordinary; but more extraordinary still is his projection of the inner turmoil of the artist, his restless search for a purpose in life."

Two more routine vehicles

GUNFIGHT AT THE O.K. CORRAL (1957). With Earl Holliman

TOP SECRET AFFAIR (1957). With Susan Hayward

followed, a rehash of the Wyatt Earp-Doc Holliday story, *Gunfight at the O.K. Corral* (1957), with Douglas playing the drunken Holliday to Burt Lancaster's Earp, and *Top Secret Affair* (1957), a romantic comedy which pitted a general played by Douglas against a flamboyant magazine publisher played by Susan Hayward. In *Gunfight at the O.K. Corral*, which suffered from the heavily prosaic directing style of John Sturges, Douglas won some praise for the conviction he brought to the Holliday role. Douglas researched the part carefully, finding that "Doc was a

meticulous dresser, but no ladies' man. He slept until noon, ate buffalo steaks, and consumed oceans of whisky." The two stars tried hard, but the film isn't within miles of the best version of the story, John Ford's *My Darling Clementine.*

Top Secret Affair was a tired, not very funny farce, directed by H. C. Potter, which poked fun at Hayward's conception of liberated womanhood and Douglas' virile strutting as a military peacock. *The Saturday Review*, calling the film "silly," observed, "Mr. Douglas' general is more believable than

Miss Hayward's publisher, but her writers may have been to blame."

Douglas tried to set up several projects in the fifties for Bryna which never reached the screen. One was *King Kelly*, in which he would have played an ex-soldier who tries to set up an empire in the Southwest after the Civil War; it would have been directed by Lewis Milestone from a Daniel Mainwaring screenplay, based on an original story by R. Wright Campbell. Another was *The Holy Circus*, about an unscrupulous evangelist (not unlike the title character of Sinclair Lewis' *Elmer Gantry*, which won Burt Lancaster his Oscar in 1959); Douglas felt the story did to religion what *Champion* did to prizefighting, but the script ran into censorship problems. Bryna invested in a play by Robert Alan Aurthur, *A Very Special Baby*, which was planned as a film project before it closed on Broadway after four performances. Douglas' publicist, Stan Margulies, commented that the flop "kept Kirk's record intact of never having any contact with a successful New York stage play—as an actor or in any other capacity."

Douglas also tried to buy the film rights to Eugene O'Neill's play *Long Day's Journey Into Night*, which Sidney Lumet filmed in 1962; he planned a Western, *The Silent Gun*, about the Colt double-action revolver, based on a televi-sion play by Carson Wiley; he had discussions with Russian officials on filming Jules Verne's novel *Michael Strogoff* in the U.S.S.R. (it would have been the first American film made there); worked on epics about the lives of Simon Bolivar and Montezuma; planned to have Robert Pirosh direct *Spring Reunion*, with Betty Hutton and Dana Andrews; developed a Borden Chase screenplay, *Viva Gringo*, which he wanted to do in a co-starring role with Rock Hudson; and also worked on a gangster film project, *A Most Contagious Game*. Other aborted projects included a film biography of Dr. Tom Dooley, the medical missionary to Indochina; a Ray Bradbury screenplay about the aftermath of atomic warfare, *And The Rock Cried Out*; *The Sun at Midnight*, an Edward Lewis script about Eskimos; and *The Indian Wars*, with an all-Indian cast.

Douglas turned down roles in *The Egyptian* and *Alexander the Great* (the latter because he would have played Philip, a secondary role to Richard Burton's Alexander), and he was interested for a time in *Heaven Knows, Mr. Allison* and *A Face in the Crowd*. He also had discussions with Billy Wilder about playing the role Tyrone Power eventually filled in *Witness for the Prosecution*.

When Douglas signed Stanley Kubrick and his partner, James

PATHS OF GLORY (1957). As Colonel Dax

Harris, to an exclusive deal with Bryna in 1957, Kubrick was only twenty-nine years old and had made three films, *Fear and Desire*, *Killer's Kiss*, and *The Killing*. The first two were low-budget, erratically promising films, and *The Killing* was an exceptionally well-done heist picture lifted far above its ostensible subject by Kubrick's inventive directing. Douglas found Kubrick, in many ways, a kindred spirit, but retained some wariness toward the younger man: "The thing that fascinates me in Stanley Kubrick," he said in the unpublished 1960 interview, "is what I call this amateurish point of view, in a healthy way, but if it goes too far it boomerangs." He also remarked that Kubrick has a "tremendous ego," and "he goes way over board — it's almost a sickness with him."

Kubrick and Harris brought Douglas a novel by Humphrey Cobb, *Paths of Glory*, which told a harshly realistic tale of chicanery among French military officers on the German front in World War I. They were having trouble finding backing for it, but succeeded with Douglas' name and the involvement of Bryna. (Douglas made a deal for 10% of the film's net profits from UA, but Bryna did not own the film, despite the production credit.)

Following his usual practice on a film which stirred his feelings, Douglas wrote Kubrick a 3500-word memo on February 13, 1957, outlining his objections to various aspects of the script. (*Paths of Glory* was written by Kubrick with Calder Willingham and Jim Thompson.) The point he made most forcefully, that the characters are too black-and-white in their morality and in the attitudes of the audience toward them, is, in retrospect, a sound criticism of the film, notwithstanding Douglas' efforts to introduce ambiguities into his role of the sympathetic officer who defends three men unjustly singled out for execution. The film, despite its undeniable brilliance, is more than a little cartoon-like; sometimes this gives it a disturbing and unusual tone of black comedy, but at other moments it makes one think of a loaded dice game.

Douglas told Kubrick that his character, Colonel Dax, was "the most lacking in depth and dimension," a "Noble Joe" whom the audience "will not like" if his character is not deepened. And Dax' antagonist, General Mireau (called Rousseau in the script, and played in the film by George Macready), was, Douglas said, "too much of an idiot":

"I cannot believe that a guy can have reached the position of general and be this kind of straight, idiotic type heavy. I say this in spite of the fact that I have absolutely no patience with professional military people. I sense an immense stupidi-

PATHS OF GLORY (1957). With Ralph Meeker

ty within them and I don't trust them. However, I must feel that within their own boundaries they know what the hell they're doing, and from the dramatic point of our story, much of our effect is lost . . . With all his faults, Rousseau must be an excellent soldier and more or less capable of dealing with his men."

In the film, Macready did indeed come out as a maniacally evil heavy, though his villainy was interestingly counterbalanced by the more subtle, and hence more insidious, evil of Adolphe Menjou as

PATHS OF GLORY (1957). With George Macready

his superior officer. Douglas played with a conviction and intelligence so palpable that the audience cannot help empathizing with his difficult position. There is, however, room for doubt as to Dax' depth of feeling, for though he argues strenuously for the men's lives, and stands up to Menjou in a memorably bitter scene, he ultimately acquiesces to the system and goes back to the front. As Douglas plays the character, he is a complicated man, far from completely admirable.

The film was a critical sensation. *The Saturday Review*, calling it "one of the screen's most extraor-

THE VIKINGS (1958). As Einar

dinary achievements," observed, "World War I seems like primitive combat in these days of ICBMs with hydrogen warheads. But there is never anything untimely about an appeal to the human conscience, and this *Paths of Glory* makes, as only one other movie I have seen makes. That was *Grand Illusion*."

While Douglas was preparing his next project for Bryna, *The Vikings*, a $3,000,000 film which eventually cost $5,000,000, Kubrick and Harris went to work on another script for him, the story of a 1920s safecracker called *I Stole $16,000,-000*. He didn't like it, nor did he go for a later script, *The German Lieutenant*, a World War II story in which Douglas would have played an heroic German. In a memo to Kubrick written by Margulies, but signed by Douglas, Kubrick was told, "This is completely a director's picture. (What else should I expect from you?) None of the roles offers any dimension, growth or challenge." Bryna's contract with Kubrick and Harris was dissolved by mutual agreement on May 1, 1958, but Douglas remained on good terms with the young director, hiring him again in 1960 to direct *Spartacus* after Anthony Mann was fired.

Of *The Vikings*, Douglas told a 1958 interviewer, "I think it's a terrific picture and if it's not, it's my own damned fault." Shot on a large scale in Norway, France, and Germany, the film was effective entertainment, full of exaggerated and corny melodrama, with a script by Calder Willingham that sometimes seems intentionally tongue-in-cheek, but subtly so, allowing the undiscriminating segments of the audience to take it as a straight-faced adventure.

Douglas prepared the film for two years, seeing it as, in Margulies' words, a commercial film which would "enable him to take a chance on another picture of questionable commercial ingredients, but which he feels strongly about." The cast, directed by Richard Fleischer, was a mugger's paradise, also including Tony Curtis as a Viking hero and Ernest Borgnine as a vicious Viking king who rampages through England like Sherman marching through Georgia. Douglas plays Borgnine's son, a warrior who goes through many outlandish battles before dying and receiving the flaming Viking funeral at the end; one of the film's most lurid scenes had Douglas losing an eye in a fight with Curtis, who is then cast into a pit of giant crabs. Douglas plays the rest of the film with a hideously distorted eye, which necessitated the wearing of a painful contact lens.

Last Train from Gun Hill (1959), reuniting Douglas with the producer (Hal Wallis) and director (John Sturges) of *Gunfight at the O.K. Corral*, was a competent

LAST TRAIN FROM GUN HILL (1959). With Earl Holliman

*THE DEVIL'S DISCIPLE (1959). With Harry Andrews, Brian Oulton, and
Laurence Olivier*

bread-and-butter Western that had
Douglas as a marshal seeking
vengeance for his wife's murder.
His nemesis in this one was
Anthony Quinn, who had played
Gauguin to his Van Gogh in *Lust
for Life.*

"*The Devil's Disciple* is not one
of (George Bernard) Shaw's best
plays, but it is better than this film
version would indicate," *Variety*
said of Douglas' next film, all the

more disappointing because it
teamed him for the first time with
Laurence Olivier, who played
Burgoyne, the stylishly villainous
British general who arouses
colonial hatred during the
American Revolution. Shaw's
waspish Irish humor seemed muted
in the film, which had Douglas as
the roguish Richard Dudgeon, help-
ing Burt Lancaster's Pastor Anderson face up to Olivier. The film, a

co-production of Bryna with Hecht-Hill-Lancaster, received middling reviews.

Douglas returned to contemporary subject matter with his next production, *Strangers When We Meet* (1960), a then-titillating Evan Hunter story of suburban adultery in which Douglas played a dynamic architect who dallies with a married woman, Kim Novak. *The Hollywood Reporter* hit the problem on the head: "A rich, juicy melodrama, dealing with the sex life of the upper middle-class, it lacks nothing that money and imagination can lavish on a motion picture, except a point of view."

STRANGERS WHEN WE MEET (1960). With Kim Novak

Ben-Hur was the big Hollywood success of 1959, cleaning up at the box office and winning eleven Oscars. Douglas wanted to play the lead, but director William Wyler preferred Charlton Heston and offered Douglas the role of Messala, which he refused. (It was played by Stephen Boyd.) Douglas' response to this blow to his ego was to make *Spartacus*, another epic about the Roman Empire: "That was what kind of spurred me to do it, in a childish way, the 'I'll-show-them' sort of thing. They can't do this to *me*. I kept thinking, if we at Bryna were doing *Ben-Hur*, I'd cast *me*, wouldn't I?"

As a further affront to the Hollywood establishment, this one stemming from nobler motives, Douglas hired blacklisted writer Dalton Trumbo to do the screenplay, causing a furor of protest from right-wing groups. "What gets me so goddam mad," Douglas said, "is I despise people who pretend that they are greater Americans than other people, sort of drape the American flag around themselves, point the finger at someone else, question the integrity of some outsider and set themselves up as a judge." Trumbo, as it turned out, wrote one of his best scripts, adapting the historical novel by Howard Fast about a slave who broke free from his Roman keepers and led a slaves' revolt against the Empire, finally being crucified.

INTO THE SIXTIES

Fast had also experienced political persecution during the blacklist period, and the story consequently had personal overtones for both writers, as well as bearing parallels to the Civil Rights movement; to Douglas, it was a perfect vehicle for his conviction that films should express meaningful social values in entertainment form, without being preachy.

"You don't often get a chance to do a movie with such a fantastic theme," he said, pointing out that the character was a complex blend of the animal and the spiritual, beginning as a brutish and brutalized sub-human and eventually finding a conscience and becoming a figure of heroic legend. Douglas, who compared the film and his struggle to make it with the story and production of *Champion*, clearly identified with Spartacus' fiery drive for independence. The book, he said, is "almost like a Horatio Alger book," though he objected to the Christ-like aura he felt surrounded Spartacus in Fast's telling of the story: "Nothing would be duller than to play a symbol."

The first budget estimate on the project was $4,000,000, and the first official estimate by Universal-International was $6,574,750, but by the time the film was completed, the total cost was between $12,000,-000 and $13,000,000, a massive

SPARTACUS (1960). With Tony Curtis

SPARTACUS (1960). With Peter Ustinov

outlay but, as Douglas pointed out, considerably less than the $16,000,000, production cost of *Ben-Hur*. U-I, which had taken on the project after United Artists rejected it, authorized the budget increases because of its excitement over the project, and over early rushes. The cast was more expensive, and better, than that of *Ben-Hur*, also including Olivier as a corrupt Roman senator, Jean Simmons as a slave girl in love with Spartacus, Tony Curtis as Olivier's favorite slave, Charles Laughton as another senator, Peter Ustinov as the head of the slave-training school, and John Gavin as Julius Caesar. Douglas originally wanted Olivier to direct but picked Mann, who had established a strong reputation with a string of superlative Westerns during the fifties.

There was a rival project in the works for a while, *The Gladiators*, which Martin Ritt was planning to direct with Yul Brynner, but it fell through, after causing Douglas considerable worry. When *Spartacus* was about to start shooting, Brynner sent Douglas a gracious cable with "all my best wishes."

The production of the epic was, as Douglas said, "a backbreaking job," entailing continual script revisions and painstaking period research, as well as marshalling the complicated resources of huge crowd and battle scenes over a 167-day shooting schedule. Mann was replaced after shooting ten days of film, some of which Kubrick redid; the film's production logs show that Mann completed just under sixteen minutes of scenes, mostly of the early sequences in the rock quarry and the gladiators' school. Though they later worked on *The Heroes of Telemark*, Mann and Douglas did not see eye-to-eye on *Spartacus*, and it was reported that Mann felt Douglas was exerting too much authority on the set. Officially, the word was that there had been "a very marked difference of opinion on many artistic matters" between the two men.

Though Kubrick today is prone to be somewhat defensive about *Spartacus*—referring to it as the only one of his films over which he did not have artistic control—it remains a superlative piece of film-making for all audiences, with a simple but far from simplistic story line and a vigorous narrative style, as well as some of the most lavish and frightening battle sequences ever put on film. Douglas gives a tightly controlled performance, both athletic and sensitive, expressing his full range as an action hero with an introspective mentality. The film had seven Oscar nominations, and won four (including Ustinov for best supporting actor), but Douglas wasn't nominated.

Dalton Trumbo also wrote the script for Douglas' next film, a

SPARTACUS (1960). Spartacus leads the slave rebellion.

moody Western called *The Last Sunset*, directed in his typically Gothic style by Robert Aldrich. Douglas was a neurotic killer, with decent instincts, who romances both Dorothy Malone and her daughter Carol Lynley while being pursued by marshal Rock Hudson. The twist in this one is that Lynley is, unbeknownst to Douglas, his own daughter, a revelation that leads Douglas to another of his suicidal deaths by gunfight. "*The Last Sunset* is a big, big Western," wrote *The Hollywood Reporter*, "but like the men it celebrates, it gives indications of being a dying breed . . . it is not an exciting picture and is particularly disappointing considering the caliber of talent that went into its acting, writing, and directing."

Town Without Pity, a 1961 film produced and directed by UA by Gottfried Reinhardt, gave Douglas the chance to reprise some elements of *Paths of Glory* in a more sensational context, but the film was not successful. He played an Army officer defending four GIs accused of raping a German girl whom Douglas winds up destroying on the witness stand, leading her to suicide. Reviewers and audiences found it "unpleasant" and not particularly insightful into either the problem of rape or the military mentality.

Lonely Are the Brave, released in 1962, remains one of Douglas' favorite films, even though some critics today find it pretentious and, in many ways, trite. It's hard to quarrel with Philip Scheuer's comment in the Los Angeles *Times* that Douglas' performance as a drifting cowboy in the contemporary West is "the most likeable portrayal he has ever given us," but it's easy to spot some of the crude symbolism and melodramatic contrivances in Dalton Trumbo's script, most blatantly the truckload of toilets which director David Miller keeps cutting to all through the film until it predictably runs down Douglas and his horse on the highway one rainy night.

The film was not commercially successful, as U-I had originally predicted when Douglas brought them Edward Abbey's book *Brave Cowboy* two years earlier; he put up completion money to get the film made, then agonized when, after receiving rave reviews, the film was allowed to die by the studio after brief initial engagements. Douglas took his case to *The New York Times*, contending, "I don't say they should spend a lot of money on it. Try it in the smaller theaters, in the art houses, so people can see it." The *Times* reporter, Murray Schumach, commented, "Critics of the handling of *Lonely Are the Brave* say it proves that the American [film] industry does not know what to do with an unusual movie and can

THE LAST SUNSET (1961). With Rock Hudson.

TOWN WITHOUT PITY (1961). With Christine Kaufmann

LONELY ARE THE BRAVE (1962). With Gena Rowlands

merely hope to blunder into a successful distribution of one."

The story, while too rhetorical to have a great appeal to action fans or Western buffs, clicked with liberals, who saw it as a protest against the dehumanizing of modern America by the forces of technology and law-and-order government, here represented by a sheriff, Walter Matthau, who uses such paraphernalia as a helicopter and walkie-talkies to track down Douglas after he escapes from his jailing on a minor charge. "I think what attracted me to the book," Douglas told *Newsweek*, "was that it had to do with a man trying to achieve freedom and how impossible it really is. *Spartacus* had the same theme. This is about enslavement in the modern age." The magazine added, "Douglas, grinning and fighting for a principle because he can't help it, is superb. The free American has never been better portrayed." But Stanley Kauffmann pointedly observed: "The film's basic shortcoming is a lack of a desirable alternative to what it seemingly deplores. Many of us uncharmed by neon and motels do not long for the old-time saloon binges and fist fights as the Lost Eden."

Two Weeks in Another Town (1962), was a severely flawed, though sporadically intriguing, insider's look at Hollywood's growing tendency at that time to make movies overseas. The principals involved in *The Bad and the Beautiful*—Douglas, producer John Houseman, director Vincente Minnelli, and writer Charles Schnee—teamed again to adapt an Irwin Shaw novel about a has-been actor (Douglas) who makes a screen comeback after recovering from a bout with booze and mental collapse. Edward G. Robinson played his director, who lets Douglas finish the film after Robinson suffers a heart attack; the newfound confidence and responsibility galvanizes Douglas' character back into strength.

Movie buffs enjoyed the film, and Peter Bogdanovich wrote an enthusiastic piece on it for *Film Culture*, but it was nowhere near the success *The Bad and the Beautiful* had been. Douglas blamed studio recutting for its weaknesses, saying the film "didn't come off." One in-joke touch that delighted the *cognoscenti* was a scene in which Douglas and Robinson screen part of *The Bad and the Beautiful* as an example of their past glory. All in all, it was a depressing, uneven rehash, lacking the bite of a cogent re-evaluation.

Douglas again returned to the subject of military responsibility with *The Hook* (1963), a lackluster film directed by George Seaton. Here, he played a sergeant in the Korean War, disturbed over orders from headquarters to execute a

LONELY ARE THE BRAVE (1962). With Michael Kane

prisoner. Though Douglas gave his "characteristically virile and authoritative performance," *Variety* commented, the film had a "tendency to stray beyond pertinent, basic issues into artificial tangents and melodramatic postures."

For Love Or Money (1963), was another minor effort, directed by Michael Gordon, which had Douglas trying comedy again as a playboy lawyer who winds up in the arms of Mitzi Gaynor after a series of romantic intrigues masterminded by her mother, Thelma Ritter. *Variety* felt that "Douglas uncorks a flair for zany comedics," but other critics disagreed, and the film doesn't hold up well.

Despite the fact that John Huston directed Douglas' next film, *The List of Adrian Messenger* (1963), it was an unsatisfactory, convoluted comedy-mystery, tediously overburdened with hammy performances by various stars in disguise, including Douglas, Frank Sinatra, Tony Curtis, Robert Mitchum, and Burt Lancaster. One amusing sidelight was that Douglas, wearing his makeup as a balding man of 65, came home one night representing himself as a *Time* reporter, fooling his cook, secretary, and maid into giving interviews about himself until his wife saw through the ruse. Generally, in more serious roles, Douglas prefers not to use heavy makeup; he felt particularly uncomfortable when the complicated logistics of *Spar-*

TWO WEEKS IN ANOTHER TOWN (1962). With Cyd Charisse

THE HOOK (1963). With Robert Walker

tacus required him to use body makeup to keep his skin a consistent color.

In the early sixties, Douglas began devoting much of his free time to a series of foreign tours on behalf of the U.S. State Department, taking him to such countries as Greece, Yugoslavia, Turkey, Israel, Thailand, India, and Japan, spreading his views of American democracy. The tours were initiated by President John F. Kennedy, who was encouraging artists to participate in a person-to-person cultural exchange program, and after a talk with Kennedy,

Douglas eagerly accepted the assignment.

"It's good for actors to do it," he commented in notes written the following year. "They like to see somebody besides a politician or a diplomat. I have a chance to be myself—go alone. And I make a point of never tying it in with a movie. If there's a picture of mine showing, I don't go. When I am under the auspices of the State Department, I try to conduct myself accordingly. Those people know a plug when they see one."

Usually, the tours produced good feeling on both sides, but there were

FOR LOVE OR MONEY (1963). With Mitzi Gaynor

THE LIST OF ADRIAN MESSENGER (1963). With George C. Scott

a few awkward incidents, one occurring when Douglas got into a heated argument with a group of what he called "Communist-inspired students" in Istanbul: "I got pretty annoyed and about twenty of them jumped over the barrier and suddenly some Turkish plainclothesmen grabbed me, threw me in a car, threw themselves on top of me, and before I knew it I was back at my hotel."

President Kennedy reciprocated the favor by giving Douglas extraordinary assistance for his next production, *Seven Days in May* (1964), an exciting melodrama about what could happen in the U.S. if civilians lost power to the military—a political theme which understandably worried Kennedy in the aftermath of the Bay of Pigs. Kennedy left the White House for his Hyannisport retreat while the film company was shooting there, and also facilitated the shooting of a scene in which a riot breaks out on the sidewalk in front of the White House. The film had no cooperation from the Pentagon, since director John Frankenheimer refused to show the script to military officials, but the film still had the look of a near-documentary, thanks in large part to Kennedy's gesture of support.

In this film adaptation of the novel by Fletcher Knebel and Charles W. Bailey, Douglas played a Marine colonel, aide to Burt Lancaster, the military chief of staff who plots a coup against President Fredric March after March negotiates a nuclear treaty with the U.S.S.R.. If anything, the film seems more plausible today, due to the revelations of military megalomania and covert plotting since the early sixties.

The film, predictably, caused agitation among many conservatives, and it was attacked on the floor of the House of Representatives by several congressmen, including Melvin Laird (R-Wis.), who would later become Secretary of Defense during the height of the Vietnam War. Laird said the film should be labeled as "fiction" when exported overseas; that he felt the warning was necessary was in itself a tribute to the film's power. One of the film's journalistic attackers, Harrison Carroll of the conservative Los Angeles *Herald-Examiner*, wrote: "The advisability of such pictures, especially for the American image abroad, is controversial. I don't think they should be made. The world is on too short a fuse."

In a low-key role beside the flashy, demonic Lancaster (also very good), Douglas added some of his customary shadings to the character, who was basically a sympathetic patriot, appalled at what Lancaster was doing. To combat the coup, Douglas has to threaten Ava Gardner, Lancaster's former

SEVEN DAYS IN MAY (1964). With Burt Lancaster

SEVEN DAYS IN MAY (1964). With Ava Gardner

IN HARM'S WAY (1965). With John Wayne

mistress, with blackmail, a highly unpleasant action which causes the character great distress. Such overtones lift the film above simple good-guys-and-bad-guys plotting, as does the expert playing of March as the rather weak president who finally acquires courage to face the threat.

The limitations of the film were in its disinclination to go one step farther and challenge the governmental system which allows the Pentagon to accumulate such dangerous power; March's speech at the end, a flag-waving oration, wrapped too neat a bow around the package and seemed highly smug and complacent in its message about democracy.

A cogent comment came from Dwight Macdonald, then the film critic for *Esquire*, who compared the film unfavorably to Kubrick's brilliant black comedy, *Dr. Strangelove*: "Politically, *Seven Days in May* is liberal, *Strangelove* is anarcho-nihilist. The former's point of view is from within existing society, and so it must take General Lancaster seriously (while the latter can spoof General Hayden) because he is the necessary evil whose blackness throws into relief the pallid virtues of President March, as the liberals built up McCarthy as a potential Hitler as a contrast to the democratic purity of Adlai Stevenson. But from a disaffected, outside standpoint, McCarthy

THE HEROES OF TELEMARK (1965). With Richard Harris

CAST A GIANT SHADOW (1966).
As Col. David (Mickey) Marcus

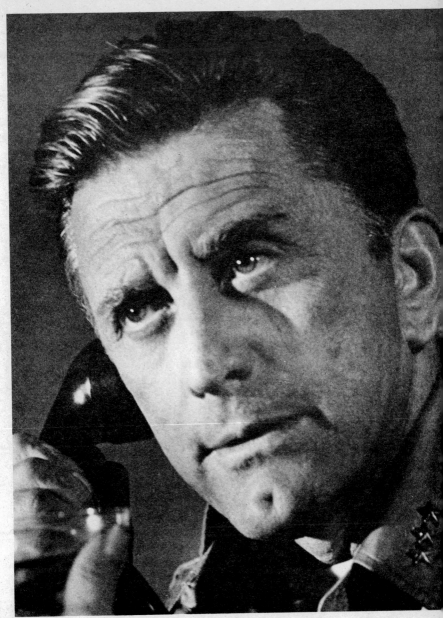

IS PARIS BURNING? (1966). As Gen. Patton

wasn't so powerful and Stevenson wasn't so pure, and both were a little ridiculous."

Somewhat incongruously, Douglas next joined John Wayne and other leading players in a war spectacle, Otto Preminger's *In Harm's Way*, which had its moments of ambivalence toward the military but generally went along with the usual overblown clichés familiar from so many previous battle epics. Douglas played an inwardly rotted Naval commander who rapes a pretty young nurse and later, wracked with guilt, undertakes a suicidal flying mission against the Japanese. Wayne and his love interest, nurse Patricia Neal, contributed fine portraits of world-weary combatants, but there was too little introspection in the midst of the spectacle, Preminger remaining content to express his cynicism with little snide moments here and there.

Little more intelligence was operative in Douglas' next film, *The Heroes of Telemark* (1965), a boring World War II adventure film in which he plays a Norwegian scientist who helps thwart German atom-bomb research. Anthony Mann, who died while making his next film, *A Dandy in Aspic*, con-tributed some of his characteristic flair for landscape, but not much else.

Douglas was greatly disappointed by the outcome of his next project, Melville Shavelson's *Cast a Giant Shadow* (1966), which, as he said, had "a wonderful subject," the life and death of Col. David (Mickey) Marcus, an American who led the Israeli defense of its land against the Arabs after the formation of Israel in 1947. "It got to be a little pretentious," Douglas comments. "It got top-heavy. I think in a sense they twisted the simplicity of the story by having all those big-name stars in it: Frank Sinatra and John Wayne and so forth." The same was true, to an even more dismaying degree, of his next film, *Is Paris Burning?* (1966), which is probably the worst film Douglas has ever made. (His subsequent film, *The Way West*, came close.) Douglas did a cameo as Gen. George S. Patton in the muddled, star-studded, totally ridiculous account of one of history's greatest dramas, the liberation of Paris in the last days of World War II. In such films, Alec Guinness has remarked with disdain, "all the audience does is spot the celebrities."

Since the mid-sixties, Douglas' credits have showed a highly erratic oscillation in quality, with the occasional peak film much rarer than in his more consistently active, more successful period from *Champion* to *Spartacus*. Even his most interesting recent films—*The Brotherhood*, *The Arrangement*, *There Was a Crooked Man*—are all, in various ways, severely flawed, and it is difficult to escape the conclusion that Douglas' career has been floundering. Now, in his sixtieth year, with his attentions turning more and more to television and to directing, it seems that, like other stars who are no longer young, Douglas is having trouble finding the right roles to fit his changing image to a changing time.

His two Westerns released in 1967, *The Way West* and *The War Wagon*, were, respectively, a preposterously botched adaptation of an A.B. Guthrie, Jr. novel and a slick piece of hokum entertainment. *The Way West* could have been a fine film, but just about everything went wrong with it, and its 122 minutes seem like an interminable parade of mistakes and clichés. Douglas plays a zealous senator who organizes a wagon train of settlers to build a utopia in Oregon; along the way, he reveals his bent towards authoritarian demagoguery, like John Wayne in Howard Hawks' *Red River*, but without that film's consistent and carefully

developed sense of time, character, and place. Under the sloppy direction of Andrew V. McLaglen, the film is a mishmash; McLaglen shows little sense of pictorial composition, blunting the effect of the landscapes, and he amuses himself by playing with his crane at every opportunity. Douglas came close to caricaturing himself in the overwrought role, particularly in a scene where he orders his black servant to whip him.

In *The War Wagon*, a considerably more accomplished film, but still a lightweight effort, Douglas is a flashy gunfighter who teams up with John Wayne in a preposterous but colorful plot to hijack an armored wagon full of gold. It was about as serious and gripping as a Saturday afternoon serial from the thirties, and one wished Wayne and Douglas could have had the chance to do a really strong Western together. But here it all went to waste, with Burt Kennedy directing strictly for easy laughs.

A Lovely Way to Die, a 1968 Universal melodrama directed by David Lowell Rich, was another forgettable excursion that did nothing to enhance Douglas' reputation. He played a rugged cop in the *Detective Story* vein—but a far less meaty characterization—who becomes a private bodyguard

THE WAY WEST (1967). With Richard Widmark

after rebelling against the new-fangled "soft" treatment of wrong-doers. That potentially interesting theme, a staple of cop movies in recent years, goes for naught here, as the film turns into a routine mystery story.

The Brotherhood, a Douglas production for Paramount about a Mafia family, was a much more personal effort, anticipating in some ways the approach Francis Ford Coppola would take in *The Godfather* three years later. Under Martin Ritt's direction, Douglas played a gutsy battler who had come up from poverty to the top of his profession—in this case, a criminal one—and then had to suffer the consequences of his overreaching ambition. Particularly engaging are the scenes in which Douglas reflects on the moral double standard of Mafia life, with its exaggerated concern for family unity in the midst of appallingly brutal "business" dealings.

The film, predictably, was attacked by the National Italian-American League to Combat Defamation, which nevertheless admitted it was "a strong story with powerful performances," and by the Americans of Italian Descent, which called it "a disgraceful spectacle that denigrates, slurs, defames, and stigmatizes twenty-two million Americans of Italian descent." Douglas also had censorship problems when some

newspapers objected to an advertising photograph showing him kissing his brother (Alex Cord) on the cheek—in the film a climactic moment just before Cord carries out an order to execute Douglas.

In an article written for the *Film and TV Daily*, Douglas commented, "I do not see any solution to the question of film censorship other than its abolition . . . Nor do I agree with the current classification of films, which is supposed to be self-regulating . . . [but] is still an attempt by a regulating body to dictate who may see what pictures."

Douglas and Elia Kazan received a barrage of hoots from the critics for *The Arrangement* (1969), but in many ways both men did some of their best work in the highly uneven film. Adapting his own best-selling novel to the screen, Kazan undoubtedly lacked perspective on the subject, which contained many autobiographical, self-critical overtones. Douglas also said he found aspects of his own life in the story of Eddie Anderson, a Los Angeles advertising executive, tired of hypocrisy and materialism, who cracks up, tries to commit suicide, and then goes on an extended freak-out ("I'm going away—into myself") in an attempt to find a new identity. Part of his problem is that he has already discarded one identity, as Evangelos Topouzoglou, son of a Greek immigrant

THE WAR WAGON (1967). With John Wayne

A LOVELY WAY TO DIE (1968). With Sharon Farrell

family, just as Douglas and Kazan had earlier changed their names and identities in seeking successful roles in American society.

The general tenor of the reviews is indicated by Pauline Kael's comments in *The New Yorker*: "It's like the slickest, ugliest, most exaggerated forties MGM movie, splintered for modernity . . . Kazan has taken forceful acting to the parody point: when Kirk Douglas and Richard Boone are on the screen together being intense—two manic, explosive specialists in the domineering-presence school of acting—two hams are trying to devour each other."

Marlon Brando was originally set to play Eddie, but dropped out for still inadequately explained reasons, and some reviewers said that Douglas failed to express the intellectual side of Eddie's nature, which they felt Brando could have conveyed. This is not a fair criticism, however, since Douglas has repeatedly demonstrated his ability to play highly intelligent characters, even if he has seldom played an intellectual. The problem, basically, was in Kazan's highly emotional rendering of the material, blotting out the more ruminative passages of the book to concentrate on Eddie's painful, near-hysteric reactions to other people. Putting Douglas and Kazan together is like shaking two highly volatile chemicals in a bottle; it's bound to produce an explosion. Another director using Douglas in a film version of *The Arrangement*—a Mankiewicz, say, or a Kubrick—could have evoked a more reflective, less completely visceral performance from him.

Certainly, the film has many moments of haunting introspection, most notably in Douglas' troubled memories of his childhood, which show him walking through vignettes of his parents and himself as a boy, wanting to reach out and comfort them but simply unable to convey his feelings, as, indeed, he is in his everyday life. The scenes with Boone, contrary to what Kael says, are devastatingly powerful pieces of acting, expertly mingling the deepest emotions of love and hate. Douglas also has some beautifully tender scenes with both Deborah Kerr, playing his wife, and Faye Dunaway, as his mistress, in the midst of lots of confused flailing-about on the part of both the character and Kazan. The film never adequately resolves Eddie's psychic dilemmas—though it concludes, movingly, on his finally tranquil smile over his father's grave—and as such remains a tantalizing failure, but still containing one of Douglas' key performances.

The scriptwriting team of David Newman and Robert Benton, having caused a sensation with their mixture of Keystone Kops comedy and brutal violence in Arthur

THE BROTHERHOOD (1968). As Frank

THE ARRANGEMENT (1969). With Deborah Kerr

Penn's 1967 landmark film, *Bonnie and Clyde*, wrote their next screenplay for director Joseph L. Mankiewicz, who cast Douglas as the title character in the oddly engaging, but far from successful, *There Was a Crooked Man* (1970). Douglas was a roguish criminal sent to the notorious Yuma, Arizona, "Hell Hole" prison near the end of the Wild West period, and the scriptwriters drew lots of black comedy from Douglas' lordly behavior in the pen and the eccentricities of his fellow inmates, including a pot-smoking old reprobate played by Burgess Meredith ("The Missouri Kid") and two quarreling homosexuals played by Hume Cronyn and John Randolph.

The cynical twists in the plot, which have Douglas getting a shocking come-uppance from a rattlesnake after he escapes to find some buried loot, were perfectly suited to Mankiewicz' drolly sophisticated style, and Douglas played with obvious relish, but the film didn't really catch on with young audiences, who still cherished a wounded idealism in 1970. Absolutely no one has any scruples in the film, even Henry Fon-

THE ARRANGEMENT (1969). With Deborah Kerr, Carol Rossen, and Anne Hegira

THERE WAS A CROOKED MAN (1970). As Paris Pitman, Jr.

A GUNFIGHT (1970). With Johnny Cash

da, a seemingly dedicated prison reformer who winds up absconding with Douglas' treasure.

The Jicarilla Indian tribe, wealthy from its oil wells and other resources, bankrolled Douglas' next film, *A Gunfight* (1971), which Bryna co-produced for MGM. Douglas and singer Johnny Cash were a pair of jaded gunslingers who decide to stage a pistol duel in a bullring for the benefit of the bloodthirsty townspeople, and to get some cash, for a change, from their gunfighting. The concept was too abstracted to make a successful film, and the hyped-up, ponderous direction by Lamont Johnson only emphasized the artificiality of the tale. But the film received some

THE LIGHT AT THE EDGE OF THE WORLD (1971). As Will Denton

critical acclaim, *Variety* noting, "In its commentary on the less-than-noble aspects of mob psychology, the film resembles *Ace in the Hole*."

The Light at the Edge of the World (1971), another Bryna coproduction, was based on a Jules Verne novel, with Douglas battling pirates in 1865 at Cape Horn, the conjunction of the Atlantic and Pacific Oceans. The film never could decide if it was designed for children or adults, and pleased neither. *Variety* considered it "good action-adventure escapism," but noted that it "might be a trifle brutal for families attracted by the GP (now PG) rating."

Michael Douglas, Kirk's oldest son, who has since become a star on television's *Streets of San Francisco* series and a successful producer with *One Flew Over the Cuckoo's Nest* (which his father unsuccessfully tried to film after playing the Jack Nicholson role on Broadway in 1963), starred in a film his father produced in 1971, *Summertree*, a contemporary drama about the problems of youth, directed by Anthony

*ONE FLEW OVER THE CUCKOO'S NEST (1963). A
publicity portrait for the Broadway stage production*

THE MASTER TOUCH (1973). With Florinda Bolkan

ONCE IS NOT ENOUGH (1975). As Mike Wayne

Newley. Kirk Douglas' third production in 1971, *Catch Me a Spy*, was a routine thriller made in Europe. Dick Clement directed Douglas as a Russian undercover agent who barely escapes the caper with his life and the love of Marlene Jobert; once again, it was formula stuff far below Douglas' talents. Later, in 1973, he appeared in another routine European-made melodrama, *A Man to Respect* (called *The Master Touch* in its sparse American release), in which he played a daredevil safecracker.

Since then, Douglas has directed *Scalawag* and *Posse*, neither of which caught on with the public; acted in two television shows, the musical *Dr. Jekyll and Mr. Hyde* (1973) and *Mousey*, the latter a pointless stunt in which he went completely against his long-established image to play a timid introvert who steps out of character to commit murder; and acted in the trashy film version of Jacqueline Susann's *Once Is Not Enough*, looking like he was ready to stalk off the set at any moment.

Anne Douglas produced *Scalawag* (1973), a G-rated pirate film teaming Douglas' salty peglegged cut-throat with moppet actor Mark Lester. The principal objection from reviewers was that it was far too violent for children (Charles Champlin of the Los Angeles *Times* said it was so gory it would "give Sam Peckinpah the shakes"), and Douglas, in retrospect, admits that he didn't know how to handle the kind of children's subject matter he and the Disney Studios had treated with such buoyant good spirits in *20,000 Leagues Under the Sea.*

By the time he made *Posse* (1975), two years later, Douglas had grown considerably more assured in his directing, and the film is a mordant, sophisticated, well-constructed Western pitting Douglas' ambitious marshal against a canny escaped criminal played by Bruce Dern. Using the Western form as a means of expressing his social preoccupations, but never succumbing to overblown rhetoric, Douglas deftly shows how his opportunist character is able to whip up the hysteria of a Texas town which eventually sees through the sham of his law-and-order credo, a cynical ploy in his plans to become a United States senator. The film lacked sensationalism, it was done in a subtly off-handed style, and it came along at a time when Westerns were still in a slough of unpopularity, so Paramount didn't put much effort into distributing it, and it died a quick death, incensing Douglas and casting doubt over his ability to sustain a directing career.

At the time of this writing, Bryna has announced its intentions to concentrate on television for a while, with projects including a

SCALAWAG (1973). As Peg

POSSE (1975). With Bruce Dern

dramatization of John Barrymore's life, starring Douglas, and a special on the life of William O. Douglas, the retired Supreme Court justice whose career has been devoted to the liberal principles Kirk Douglas has always admired. As late as 1963, Douglas spoke disparagingly of working in television, but now it seems a necessity.

Douglas' comment at the end of his 1957 autobiographical article seems appropriate to recall at this juncture in his career: "I've been lucky enough to make a few good pictures, but I don't assume I'll never boot one. No one bats a thousand in any league, and a champ is a guy who walks into the ring one day and gets clobbered by a kid no one ever heard of. All I can do is work as hard as I know how, and, when the chips are down, gamble on myself."

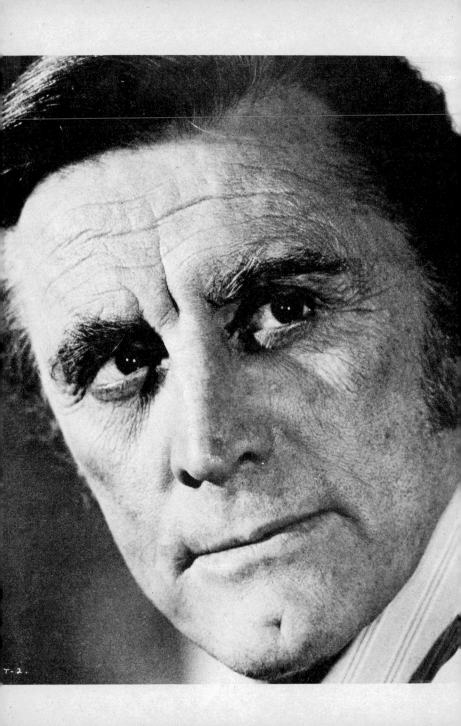

BIBLIOGRAPHY

Arneel, Gene. "Look, Ma, I'm a Corporation," *Variety,* March 16, 1955.

Douglas, Anne. "My Awful Wedded Husband," *The Saturday Evening Post,* November 24, 1962.

Douglas, Kirk, as told to Pete Martin. "The Actor in Me," *The Saturday Evening Post,* June 22, 1957, and June 29, 1957.

Gow, Gordon. "Impact," an interview with Kirk Douglas, *Films and Filming,* September, 1972.

Porter, Sylvia. "You — A 'Corporation'?," The New York *Post,* April 5, 1955.

Redbook magazine. *"Redbook* Readers Talk with Kirk Douglas," April, 1966.

Thomas, Tony. *The Films of Kirk Douglas,* The Citadel Press, Secaucus, N.J., 1972.

THE FILMS OF KIRK DOUGLAS

The director's name follows the release date. A (c) following the release date indicates that the film was in color. Sp indicates Screenplay, and b/o indicates based on.

1. THE STRANGE LOVE OF MARTHA IVERS. Paramount, 1946. *Lewis Milestone.* Sp: Robert Rossen, b/o story by Jack Patrick. Cast: Barbara Stanwyck, Van Heflin, Lizabeth Scott, Judith Anderson, Roman Bohnen, Darryl Hickman.

2. OUT OF THE PAST. RKO, 1947. *Jacques Tourneur.* Sp: Geoffrey Homes, b/o his novel "Build My Gallows High." Cast: Robert Mitchum, Jane Greer, Rhonda Fleming, Richard Webb, Steve Brodie, Virginia Huston.

3. MOURNING BECOMES ELECTRA. RKO, 1947. *Dudley Nichols.* Sp: Dudley Nichols, b/o play by Eugene O'Neill. Cast: Rosalind Russell, Michael Redgrave, Raymond Massey, Katina Paxinou, Leo Genn, Nancy Coleman.

4. I WALK ALONE. Paramount, 1947. *Byron Haskins.* Sp: Charles Schnee, adapted by Robert Smith and John Bright, b/o play "The Beggars Are Coming To Town" by Theodore Reeves. Cast: Burt Lancaster, Lizabeth Scott, Wendell Corey, Kristine Miller.

5. THE WALLS OF JERICHO. 20th Century-Fox, 1948. *John M. Stahl.* Sp: Lamar Trotti, b/o novel by Paul Wellman. Cast: Cornel Wilde, Linda Darnell, Anne Baxter, Ann Dvorak, Colleen Townsend, Marjorie Rambeau.

6. MY DEAR SECRETARY. A Harry M. Popkin Production, released by United Artists, 1948. *Charles Martin.* Sp: Charles Martin. Cast: Laraine Day, Keenan Wynn, Helen Walker, Rudy Vallee.

7. A LETTER TO THREE WIVES. 20th Century-Fox, 1948. *Joseph L. Mankiewicz.* Sp: Joseph L. Mankiewicz, adapted by Vera Caspary from the story by John Klempner. Cast: Jeanne Crain, Linda Darnell, Ann Sothern, Paul Douglas, Barbara Lawrence, Jeffrey Lynn.

8. CHAMPION. A Stanley Kramer Production, released by United Artists, 1949. *Mark Robson.* Sp: Carl Foreman, b/o story by Ring Lardner. Cast: Marilyn Maxwell, Arthur Kennedy, Paul Stewart, Ruth Roman, Lola Albright.

9. YOUNG MAN WITH A HORN. Warner Bros., 1950. *Michael Curtiz.* Sp: Carl Foreman, Edmund H. North, b/o novel by Dorothy Baker. Cast: Lauren Bacall, Doris Day, Hoagy Carmichael, Juano Hernandez, Jerome Cowan, Mary Beth Hughes.

10. THE GLASS MENAGERIE. Warner Bros., 1950. *Irving Rapper.* Sp: Tennessee Williams, Peter Berneis, b/o Williams' play. Cast: Jane Wyman, Gertrude Lawrence, Arthur Kennedy.

11. ACE IN THE HOLE. Paramount, 1951. *Billy Wilder.* Sp: Billy Wilder, Lesser Samuels, Walter Newman. Cast: Jan Sterling, Bob Arthur, Porter Hall, Richard Benedict, Frank Cady, Ray Teal.

12. ALONG THE GREAT DIVIDE. Warner Bros., 1951. *Raoul Walsh.* Sp: Walter Doniger, Lewis Meltzer, b/o story by Doniger. Cast: Virginia Mayo, John Agar, Walter Brennan, Ray Teal.

13. DETECTIVE STORY. Paramount, 1951. *William Wyler.* Sp: Philip Yordan, Robert Wyler, b/o play by Sidney Kingsley. Cast: Eleanor Parker, William Bendix, Horace McMahon, Lee Grant, Bert Freed, Craig Hill, Cathy O'Donnell.

14. THE BIG TREES. Warner Bros., 1952 (c). *Felix Feist.* Sp: John Twist, James R. Webb, b/o story by Kenneth Earl. Cast: Eve Miller, Patrice Wymore, Edgar Buchanan, John Archer, Alan Hale, Jr.

15. THE BIG SKY. RKO, 1952. *Howard Hawks.* Sp: Dudley Nichols, b/o novel by A. B. Guthrie, Jr. Cast: Dewey Martin, Elizabeth Threatt, Arthur Hunnicutt, Buddy Baer, Steven Geray, Hank Worden.

16. THE BAD AND THE BEAUTIFUL. MGM, 1952. *Vincente Minnelli,* Sp: Charles Schnee, b/o story by George Bradshaw. Cast: Lana Turner, Walter Pidgeon, Dick Powell, Barry Sullivan, Gloria Grahame, Gilbert Roland.

17. THE STORY OF THREE LOVES (EQUILIBRIUM episode). MGM 1953 (c). *Gottfried Reinhardt.* Sp: John Collier, adapted by Jan Lustig and George Froeschel from story by Ladislas Vajda. Cast: Pier Angeli, Richard Anderson.

18.   THE JUGGLER. A Stanley Kramer Production, released by Columbia, 1953. *Edward Dmytryk.* Sp: Michael Blankfort, b/o his novel. Cast: Milly Vitale, Paul Stewart, Joey Walsh, Alf Kjellin, Beverly Washburn.

19.   ACT OF LOVE. A Benagoss Production, released by United Artists, 1953. *Anatole Litvak.* Sp: Irwin Shaw, b/o novel by Alfred Hayes. Cast: Dany Robin, Barbara Laage, Robert Strauss, Gabrielle Dorziat.

20.   ULYSSES. A Lux Films-Ponti-De Laurentiis Production, released by Paramount, 1954. *Mario Camerini.* Sp: Franco Brusati, Mario Camerini, Enio de Concini, Hugh Gray, Ben Hecht, Ivo Perilli, and Irwin Shaw, b/o Homer's "Odyssey." Cast: Silvana Mangano, Anthony Quinn, Rossana Podesta, Sylvie.

21.   20,000 LEAGUES UNDER THE SEA. A Walt Disney Production, released by Buena Vista, 1954 (c). *Richard Fleischer.* Sp: Earl Fenton, b/o book by Jules Verne. Cast: James Mason, Paul Lukas, Peter Lorre, Robert J. Wilke, Carleton Young, Ted de Corsia.

22.   THE RACERS. 20th Century-Fox, 1955 (c). *Henry Hathaway.* Sp: Charles Kaufman, b/o novel by Hans Reusch. Cast: Bella Darvi, Gilbert Roland, Cesar Romero, Lee J. Cobb, Katy Jurado.

23.   MAN WITHOUT A STAR. Universal, 1955 (c). *King Vidor.* Sp: Borden Chase, D. D. Beauchamp, b/o novel by Dee Linford. Cast: Jeanne Crain, Claire Trevor, William Campbell, Richard Boone, Mara Corday, J. C. Flippen.

24.   THE INDIAN FIGHTER. A Bryna Production, released by United Artists, 1955 (c). *Andre de Toth.* Sp: Frank Davis, Ben Hecht, b/o story by Ben Kadish. Cast: Elsa Martinelli, Walter Abel, Walter Matthau, Diana Douglas, Eduard Franz, Lon Chaney.

25.   LUST FOR LIFE. MGM, 1956 (c). *Vincente Minnelli.* Sp: Norman Corwin, b/o novel by Irving Stone. Cast: Anthony Quinn, James Donald, Pamela Brown, Everett Sloane, Niall MacGinnis, Noel Purcell.

26.   GUNFIGHT AT THE O.K. CORRAL. Paramount, 1957 (c). *John Sturges.* Sp: Leon Uris. Cast: Burt Lancaster, Rhonda Fleming, Jo Van Fleet, John Ireland, Lyle Bettger, Earl Holliman, Frank Faylen.

27.   TOP SECRET AFFAIR. Warner Bros., 1957. *H. C. Potter.* Sp: Roland Kibbee, Allan Scott, b/o characters in "Melville Goodwin, U.S.A." by John P. Marquand. Cast: Susan Hayward, Paul Stewart, Jim Backus, John Cromwell, Roland Winters.

28. PATHS OF GLORY. A Bryna Production, released by United Artists, 1957. *Stanley Kubrick.* Sp: Stanley Kubrick, Calder Willingham, Jim Thompson, b/o novel by Humphrey Cobb. Cast: Ralph Meeker, Adolphe Menjou, George Macready, Wayne Morris, Richard Anderson, Joseph Turkel.

29. THE VIKINGS. A Kirk Douglas Production, released by United Artists, 1958 (c). *Richard Fleischer.* Sp: Calder Willingham, adapted by Dale Wasserman from novel "The Viking" by Edison Marshall. Cast: Tony Curtis, Ernest Borgnine, Janet Leigh, James Donald, Alexander Knox, Frank Thring.

30. LAST TRAIN FROM GUN HILL. Paramount, 1959 (c). *John Sturges.* Sp: James Poe, b/o story by Les Crutchfield. Cast: Anthony Quinn, Carolyn Jones, Earl Holliman, Brad Dexter, Ziva Rodann.

31. THE DEVIL'S DISCIPLE. A Brynaprod, S. A. and Hecht-Hill-Lancaster Films, Ltd. Production, released by United Artists, 1959. *Guy Hamilton.* Sp: John Dighton, Roland Kibbee, b/o play by George Bernard Shaw. Cast: Burt Lancaster, Laurence Olivier, Janette Scott, Eva Le Gallienne, Harry Andrews, George Rose.

32. STRANGERS WHEN WE MEET. Columbia, 1960 (c). *Richard Quine.* Sp: Evan Hunter, b/o his novel. Cast: Kim Novak, Ernie Kovacs, Barbara Rush, Walter Matthau, Virginia Bruce, Kent Smith, Helen Gallagher.

33. SPARTACUS. A Bryna Production, released by Universal-International, 1960 (c). *Stanley Kubrick.* Sp: Dalton Trumbo, b/o novel by Howard Fast. Cast: Laurence Olivier, Jean Simmons, Tony Curtis, Charles Laughton, Peter Ustinov, John Gavin, Nina Foch.

34. THE LAST SUNSET. Universal-International, 1961 (c). *Robert Aldrich.* Sp: Dalton Trumbo, b/o novel "Sundown At Crazy Horse" by Howard Rigsby. Cast: Rock Hudson, Dorothy Malone, Joseph Cotten, Carol Lynley, Neville Brand, Regis Toomey.

35. TOWN WITHOUT PITY. A Mirisch Company–Gloria Film Production, released by United Artists, 1961. *Gottfried Reinhardt.* Sp: Silvia Reinhardt, Georg Hurdalek, b/o the novel "The Verdict" by Manfred Gregor. Cast: Christine Kaufmann, E. G. Marshall, Robert Blake, Richard Jaeckel, Hans Nielsen, Karin Hardt.

36. LONELY ARE THE BRAVE. An Edward Lewis Production, released by Universal-International, 1962. *David Miller.* Sp: Dalton Trumbo, b/o novel "Brave Cowboy" by Edward Abbey. Cast: Gena Rowlands, Walter Matthau, Michael Kane, Carroll O'Connor.

37. TWO WEEKS IN ANOTHER TOWN. MGM, 1962 (c). *Vincente Minnelli.* Sp: Charles Schnee, b/o novel by Irwin Shaw. Cast: Edward G. Robinson, Cyd Charisse, George Hamilton, Dahlia Lavi, Claire Trevor.

38. THE HOOK. MGM, 1963. *George Seaton.* Sp: Henry Denker, b/o novel "L'Hamecon" by Vahe Katcha. Cast: Robert Walker, Nick Adams, Enrique Magalona, Nehemiah Persoff.

39. FOR LOVE OR MONEY. Universal-International, 1963 (c). *Michael Gordon.* Sp: Larry Markes, Michael Morris. Cast: Mitzi Gaynor, Gig Young, Thelma Ritter, Leslie Parrish, Julie Newmar.

40. THE LIST OF ADRIAN MESSENGER. A Joel Production, released by Universal, 1963. *John Huston.* Sp: Anthony Veiller, b/o novel by Philip MacDonald. Cast: George C. Scott, Dana Wynter, Clive Brook, Herbert Marshall, Jacques Roux.

41. SEVEN DAYS IN MAY. Paramount, 1964. *John Frankenheimer.* Sp: Rod Serling, b/o novel by Fletcher Knebel, Charles W. Bailey. Cast: Burt Lancaster, Fredric March, Ava Gardner, Edmond O'Brien, Martin Balsam, George Macready.

42. IN HARM'S WAY. An Otto Preminger Production, released by Paramount, 1965. *Otto Preminger.* Sp: Wendell Mayes, b/o novel by James Bassett. Cast: John Wayne, Patricia Neal, Henry Fonda, Tom Tryon, Paula Prentiss, Brandon de Wilde, Jill Haworth, Dana Andrews.

43. THE HEROES OF TELEMARK. Columbia, 1965 (c). *Anthony Mann.* Sp: Ivan Moffat, Ben Barzman, b/o "Skis Against the Atom" by Knut Haukelid and "But For These Men" by John Drummond. Cast: Richard Harris, Ulla Jacobsson, Michael Redgrave, David Weston, Anton Diffring, Mervyn Johns.

44. CAST A GIANT SHADOW. A Mirisch-Lienroc-Batjac Production, released by United Artists, 1966 (c). *Melville Shavelson.* Sp: Melville Shavelson, from book by Ted Berkman. Cast: Senta Berger, Angie Dickinson, James Donald, Stathis Giallelis, Yul Brynner, John Wayne, Frank Sinatra.

45. IS PARIS BURNING? Paramount, 1966. *Rene Clement.* Sp: Gore Vidal, Francis Ford Coppola, b/o book by Larry Collins and Dominique Lapierre. Cast: star cameos.

46. THE WAY WEST. A Harold Hecht Production, released by United Artists, 1967 (c). *Andrew V. McLaglen.* Sp: Ben Maddow, Mitch Lindemann, b/o novel by A. B. Guthrie, Jr. Cast: Robert Mitchum, Richard Widmark, Lola Albright, Michael Witney, Stubby Kaye, Sally Field.

47. THE WAR WAGON. A Batjac Production, released by Universal International, 1967 (c). *Burt Kennedy.* Sp: Claire Huffaker, b/o his novel "Badman." Cast: John Wayne, Howard Keel, Robert Walker, Keenan Wynn, Bruce Cabot.

48. A LOVELY WAY TO DIE. Universal, 1968 (c). *David Lowell Rich.* Sp: A. J. Russell. Cast: Sylva Koscina, Eli Wallach, Kenneth Haigh, Martyn Green, Sharon Farrell.

49. THE BROTHERHOOD. A Kirk Douglas Production, released by Paramount, 1969 (c). *Martin Ritt.* Sp: Lewis John Carlino. Cast: Alex Cord, Irene Papas, Luther Adler, Susan Strasberg, Murray Hamilton, Eduardo Ciannelli.

50. THE ARRANGEMENT. An Elia Kazan Production, released by Warner Bros., 1969 (c). *Elia Kazan.* Sp: Elia Kazan, b/o his novel. Cast: Faye Dunaway, Deborah Kerr, Richard Boone, Hume Cronyn, Michael Higgins, Carol Rossen.

51. THERE WAS A CROOKED MAN. Warner Bros.–7 Arts, 1970 (c). *Joseph L. Mankiewicz.* Sp: David Newman, Robert Benton. Cast: Henry Fonda, Hume Cronyn, Warren Oates, Burgess Meredith, Arthur O'Connell, Martin Gabel.

52. A GUNFIGHT. A Harvest–Thoroughbred–Bryna Production, released by MGM, 1971 (c). *Lamont Johnson.* Sp: Harold Jack Bloom. Cast: Johnny Cash, Jane Alexander, Raf Vallone, Karen Black, Eric Douglas, Phillip Mead.

53. THE LIGHT AT THE EDGE OF THE WORLD. A Bryna–Jet Films, S.A., and Triumfilm Production, released by National General, 1971 (c). *Kevin Billington.* Sp: Tom Rowe, b/o novel by Jules Verne. Cast: Yul Brynner, Samantha Eggar, Jean Claude Drouot, Fernando Rey.

54. CATCH ME A SPY. A Ludgate Films – Capitole Films – Bryna Production, released by Rank, 1971 (c). *Dick Clement.* Sp: Dick Clement, Ian La Frenais, b/o novel by George Marton and Tibor Meray. Cast: Marlene Jobert, Trevor Howard, Tom Courtenay, Patrick Mower, Bernard Blier.

55. THE MASTER TOUCH (A MAN TO RESPECT). Warner Bros., 1973 (c). *Michele Lupo*. Sp: Mino Roli, Franco Bucceri, Roberto Leoni, and Michele Lupo. Cast: Florinda Bolkan, Giuliano Gemma, Rene Koldehoff, Wolfgang Preiss.

56. SCALAWAG. An Inex-Oceania-Bryna (Anne Douglas) Production, released by Paramount, 1973 (c). *Kirk Douglas*. Sp: Albert Maltz, Sid Fleischman, b/o story by Robert Louis Stevenson. Cast: Mark Lester, Neville Brand, George Eastman, Don Stroud, Lesley Anne Down.

57. POSSE. A Bryna Production, released by Paramount, 1975 (c). *Kirk Douglas*. Sp: William Roberts, Christopher Knopf, b/o story by Knopf. Cast: Bruce Dern, Bo Hopkins, James Stacy, Luke Askew, David Canary.

58. ONCE IS NOT ENOUGH. Paramount, 1975 (c). *Guy Green*. Sp: Julius J. Epstein, b/o novel by Jacqueline Susann. Cast: Alexis Smith, David Janssen, George Hamilton, Deborah Raffin, Brenda Vaccaro, Gary Conway.

INDEX

ABOUT THE AUTHOR

A critic/reporter for *Variety*, Joseph McBride is the author of *Orson Welles*, co-author of *John Ford*, and editor of *Focus on Howard Hawks* and *Persistence of Vision*. Among the film magazines to which he has contributed are *Sight and Sound, American Film, Film Comment, Film Heritage, The Silent Picture*, and *The Velvet Light Trap*. He has also appeared in several films, including *The Other Side of the Wind, The Wild Party*, and *Hollywood Boulevard*.

ABOUT THE EDITOR

Ted Sennett is the author of *Warner Brothers Presents*, a tribute to the great Warners films of the thirties and forties, and of *Lunatics and Lovers*, on the long-vanished but well-remembered "screwball" movie comedies of the past. He is also the editor of *The Movie Buff's Book* and has written about films for magazines and newspapers. He lives in New Jersey with his wife and three children.